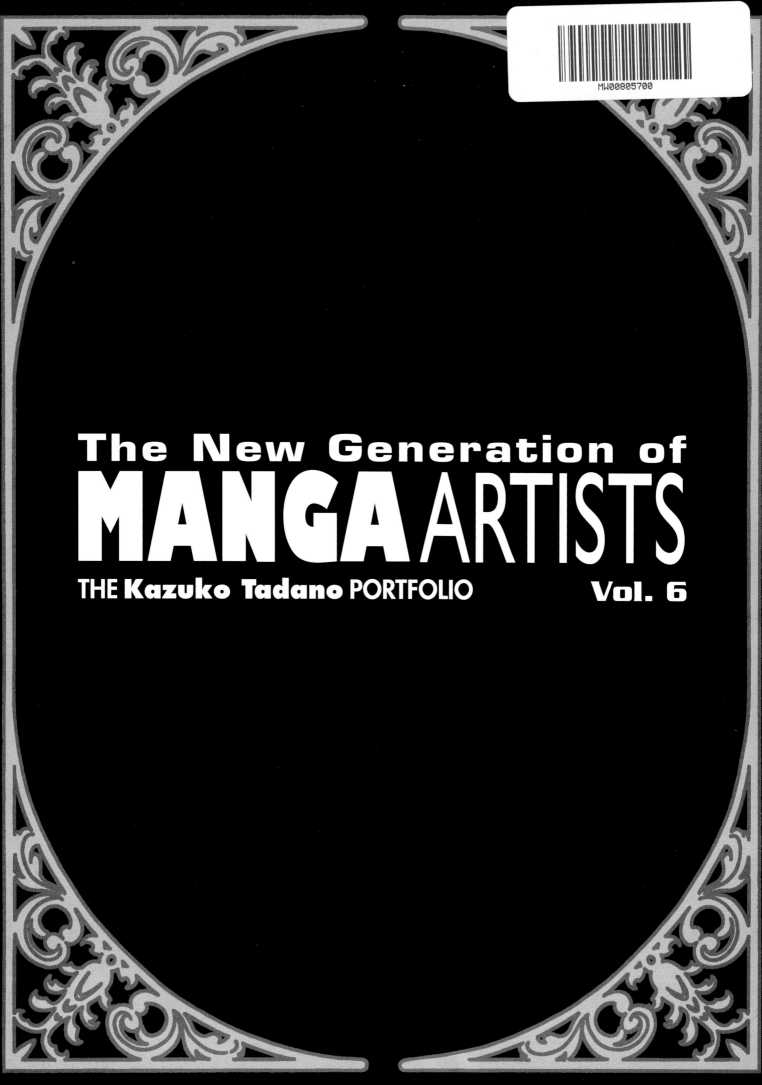

The New Generation of
MANGA ARTISTS

THE Kazuko Tadano PORTFOLIO

Vol. 6

THE NEW GENERATAION OF MANGA ARTISTS
VOL. 6: The Kazuko Tadano Portfolio

Copyright © 2004 Kazuko Tadano
Copyright © 2004 Graphic-sha Publishing Co., Ltd.

This book was first designed and published in Japan in 2004 by Graphic-sha Publishing Co., Ltd.
This English edition was published in 2004 by Graphic-sha Publishing Co., Ltd.
Sansou Kudan Bldg. 4th Floor, 1-14-17 Kudan-kita, Chiyoda-ku, Tokyo 102-0073 Japan

Original cover design and text pag layout:	Shinichi Ishioka
English translation management:	Língua fránca, Inc. (an3y-skmt@asahi-net.or.jp)
Planning editor:	Kuniyoshi Masujima (Graphic-sha Publishing Co., Ltd.)
Publishing coordinator:	Michiko Yasu (Graphic-sha Publishing Co., Ltd.)
Project management:	Kumiko Sakamoto (Graphic-sha Publishing Co., Ltd.)

First printing: October 2004

ISBN: 4-7661-1468-X
Printed and bound in China by Everbest Printing Co., Ltd.

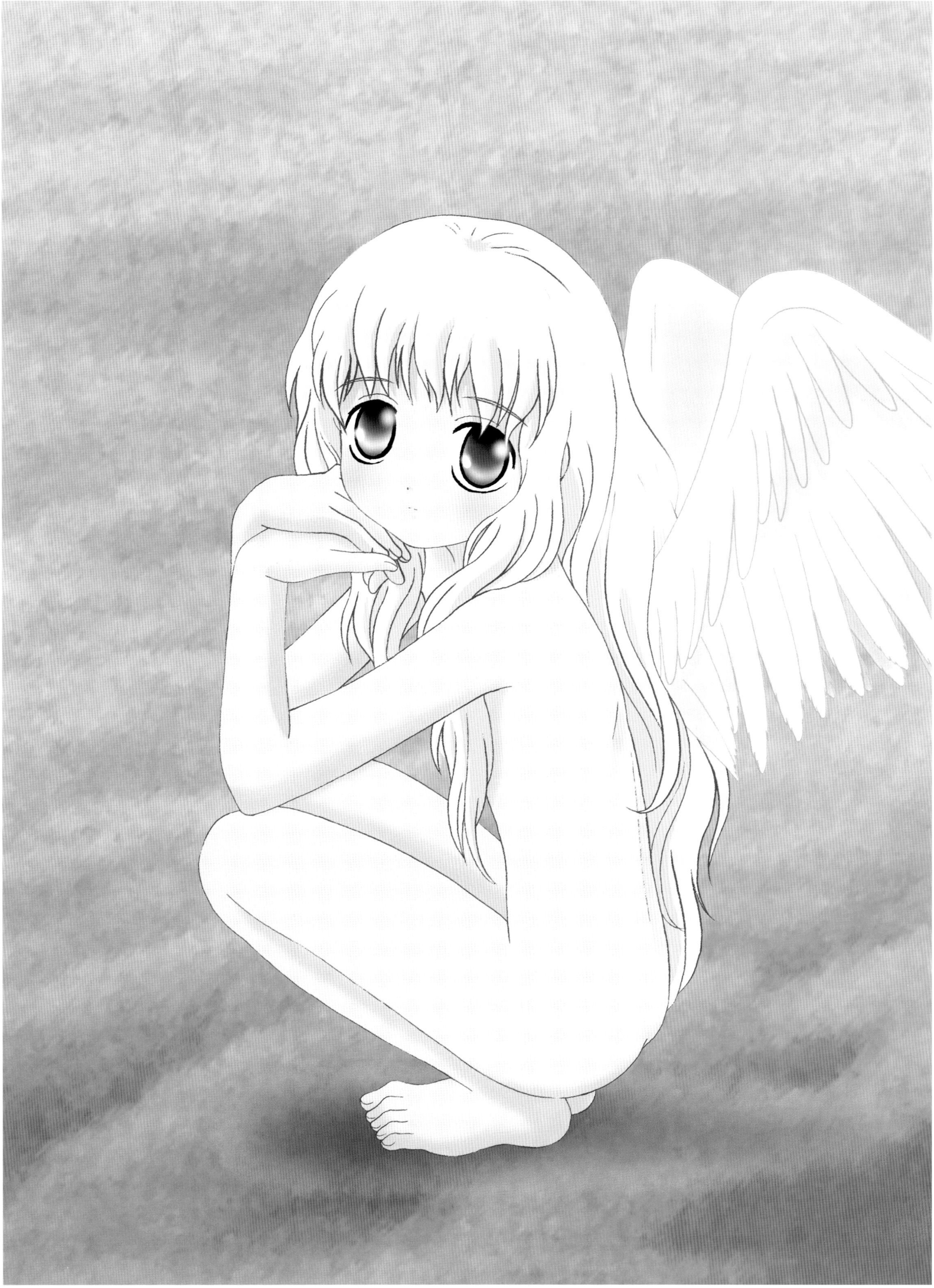

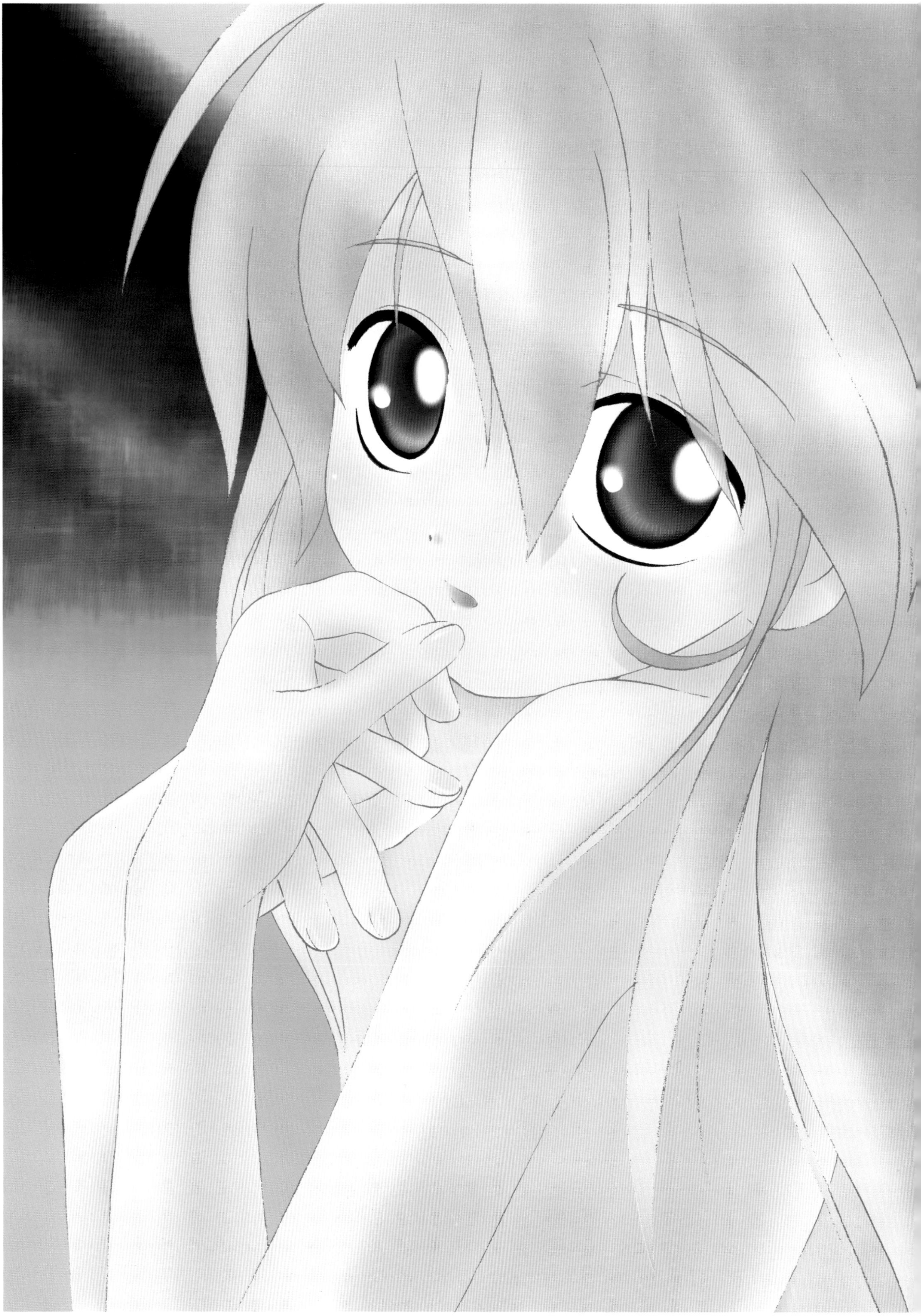

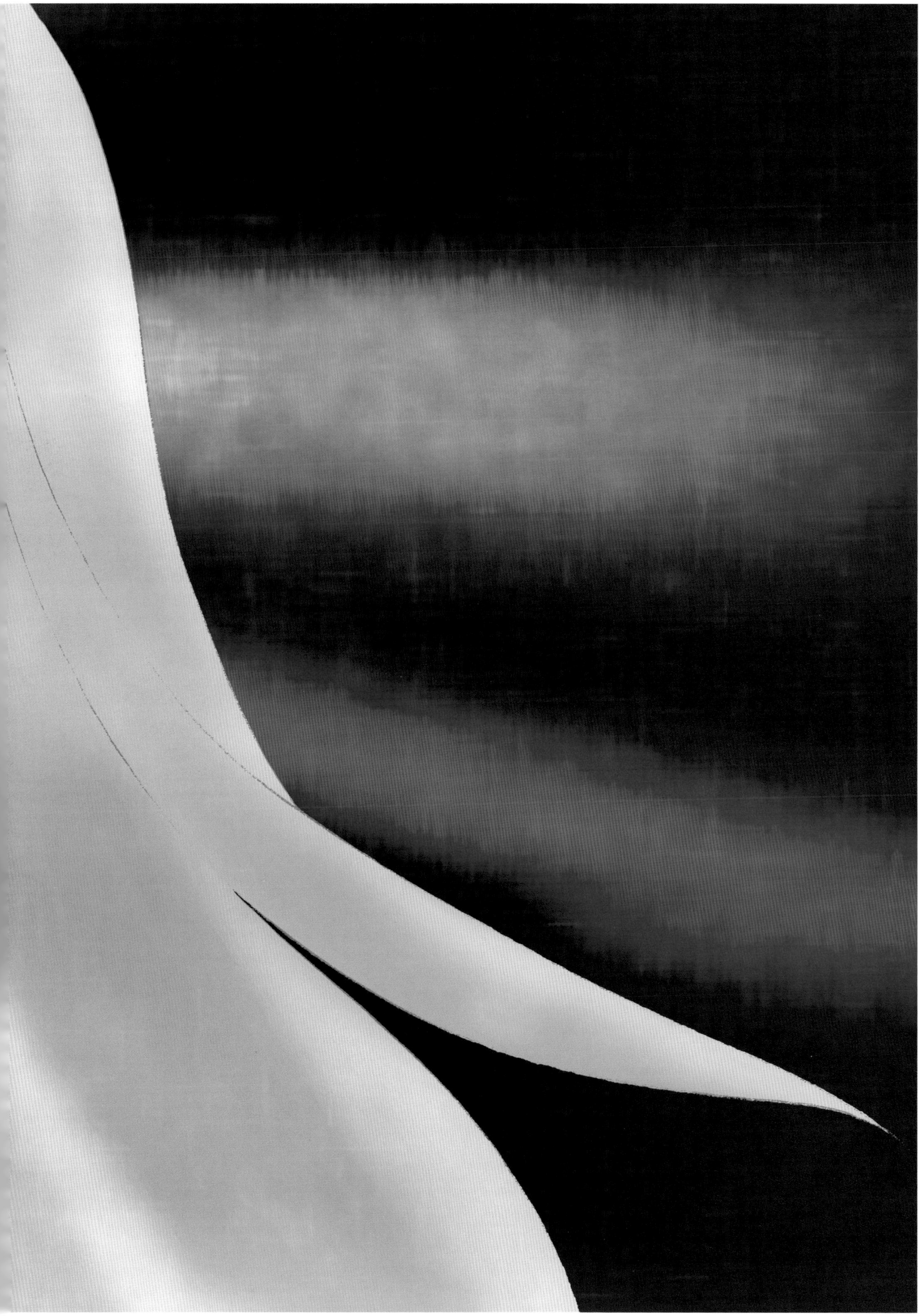

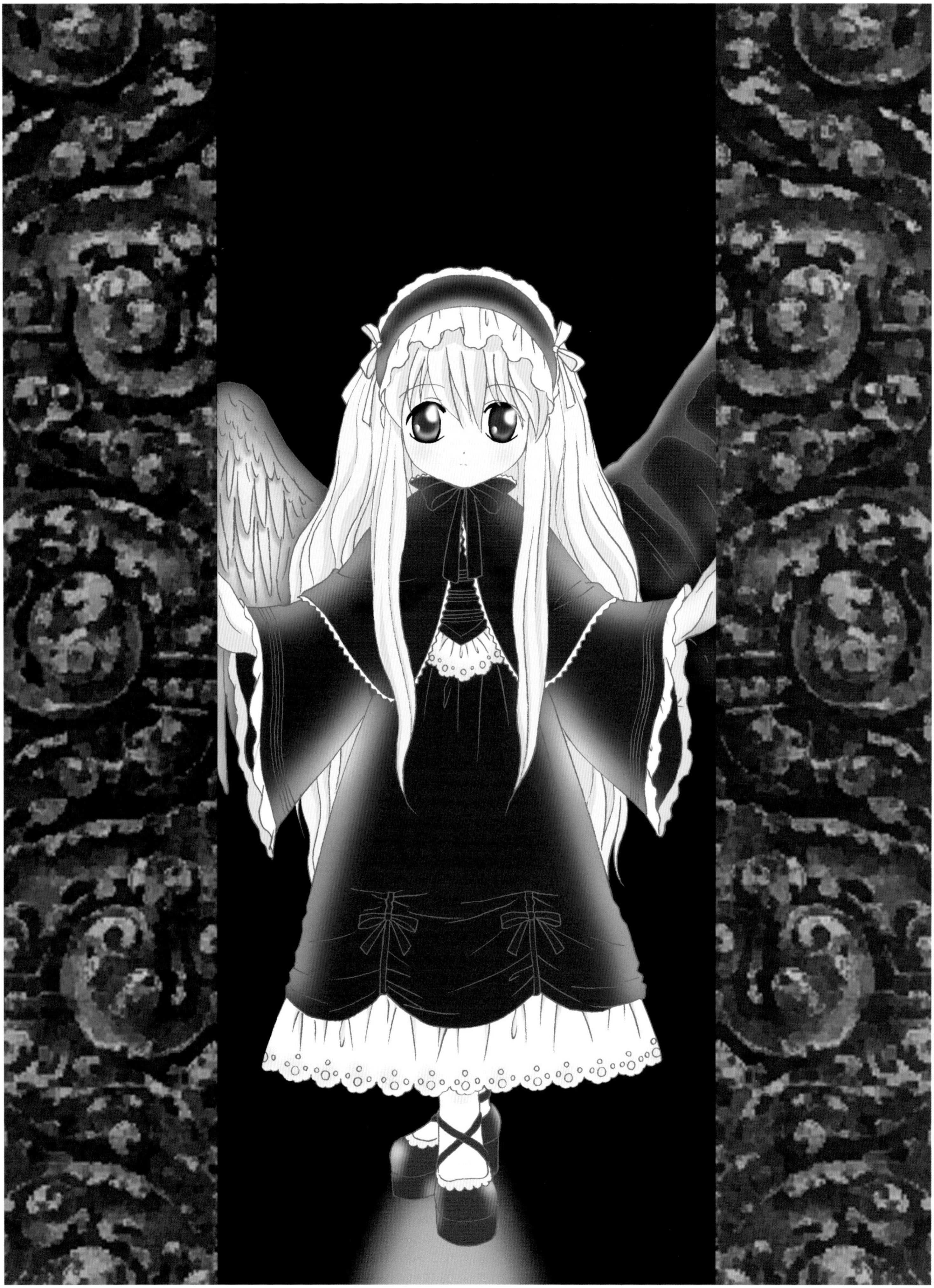

Karen Sugisaki

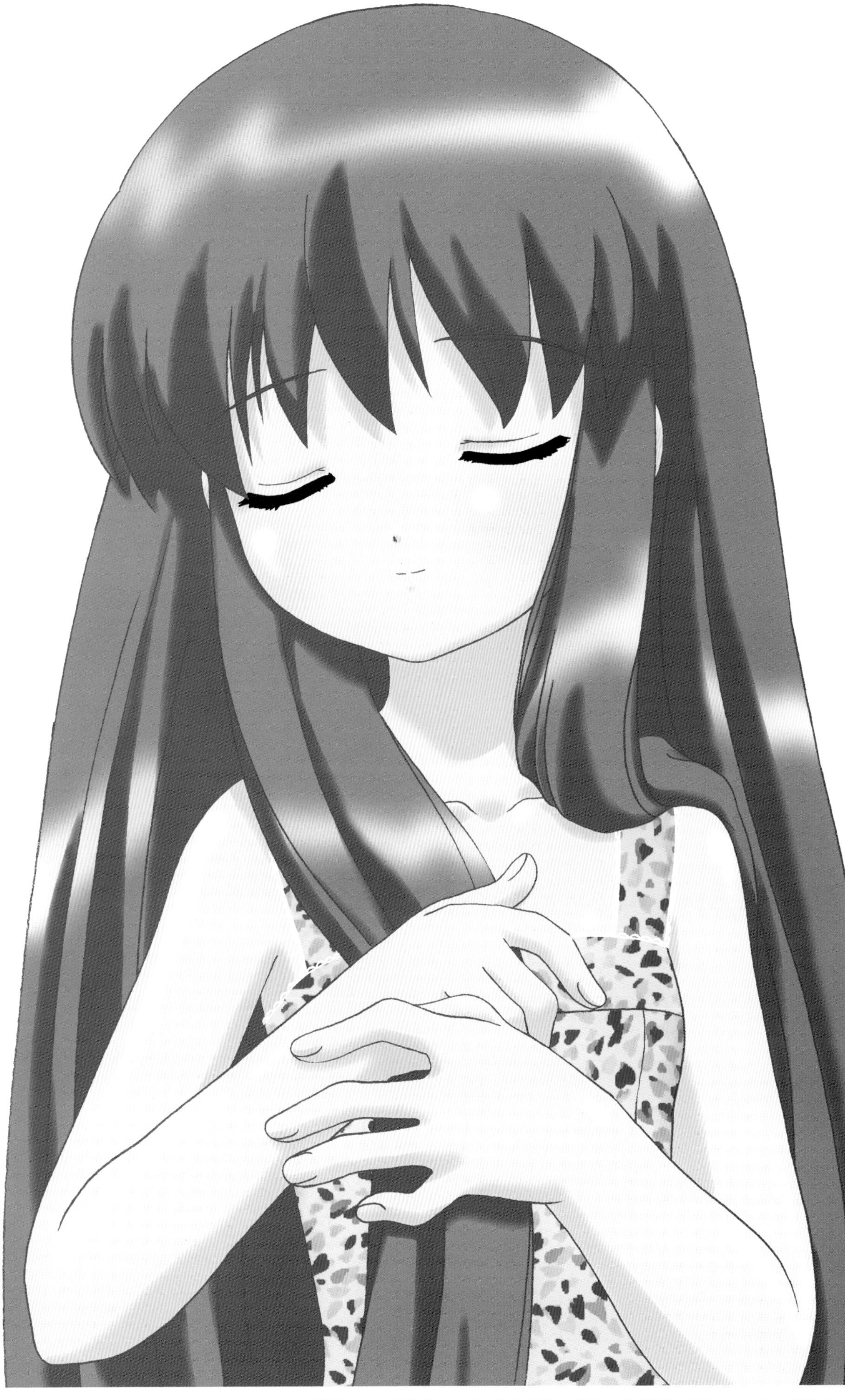

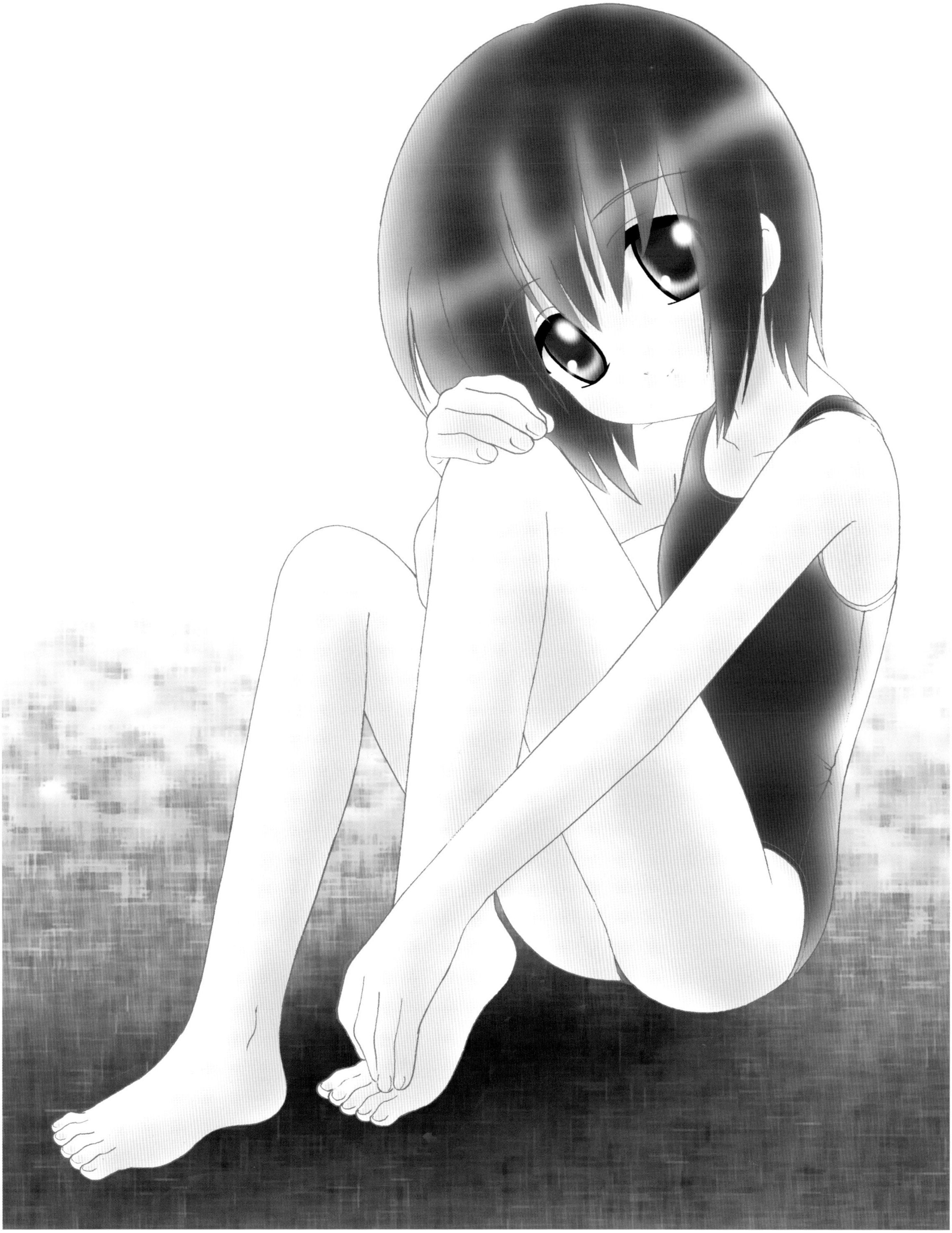

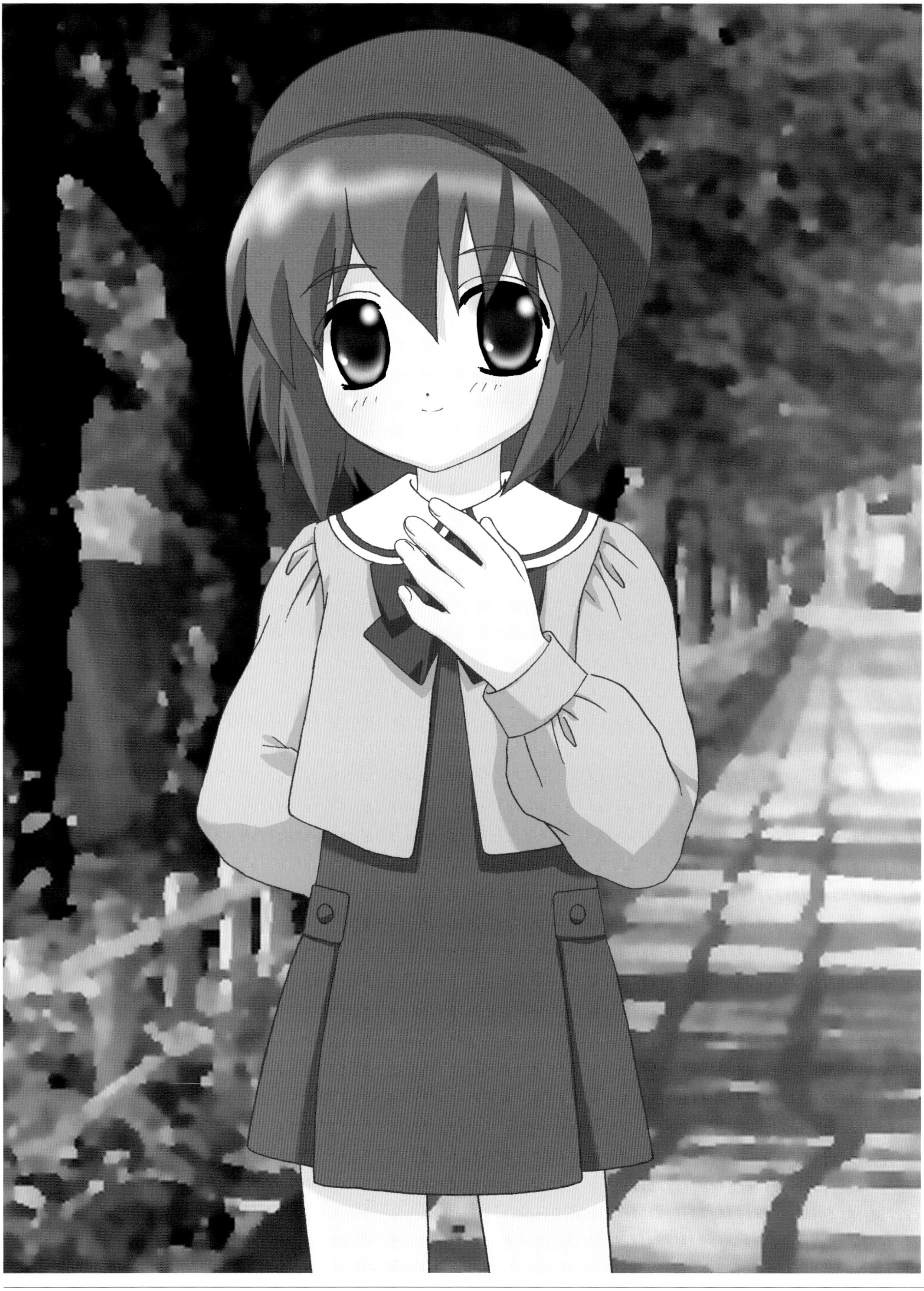

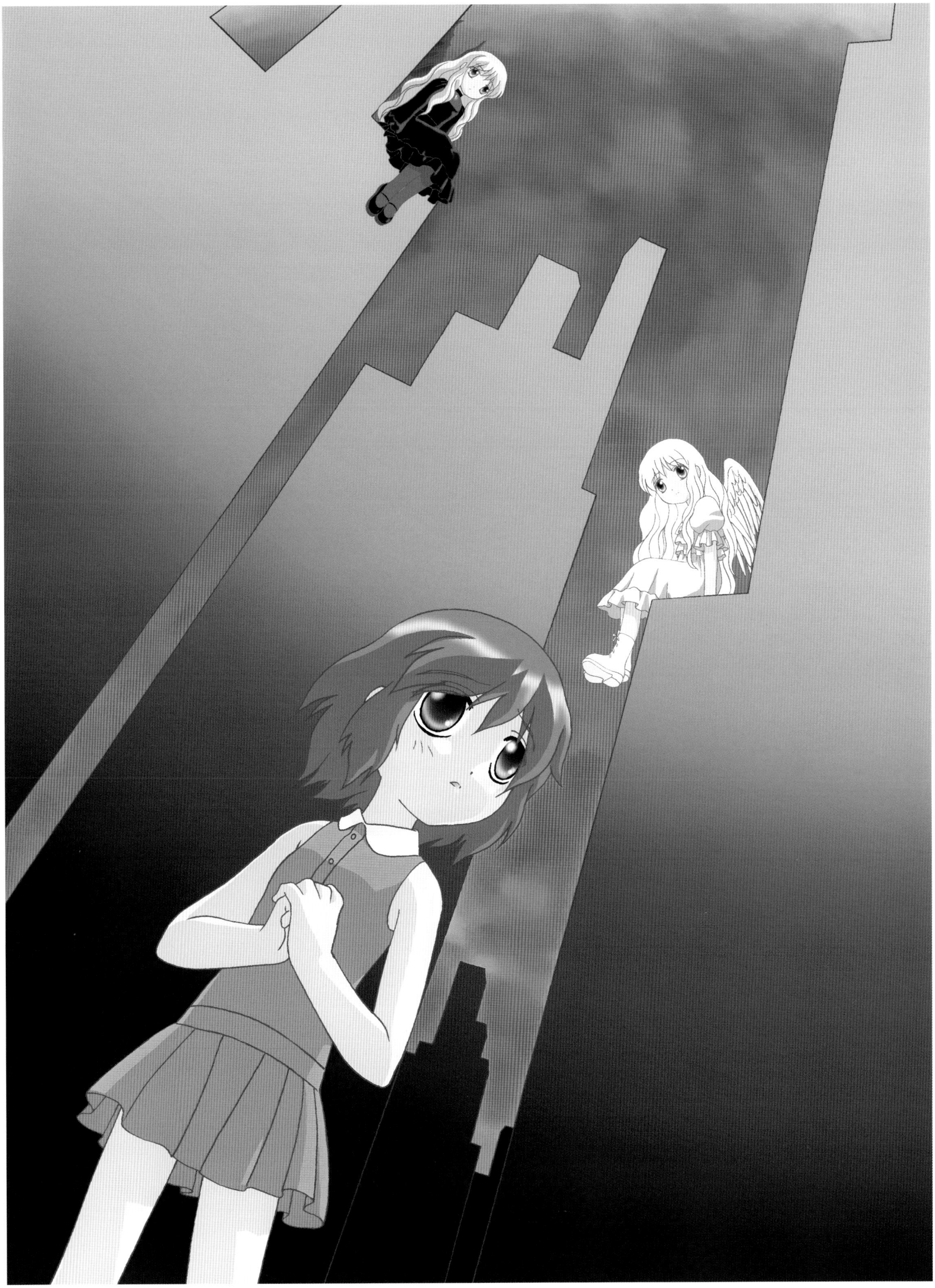

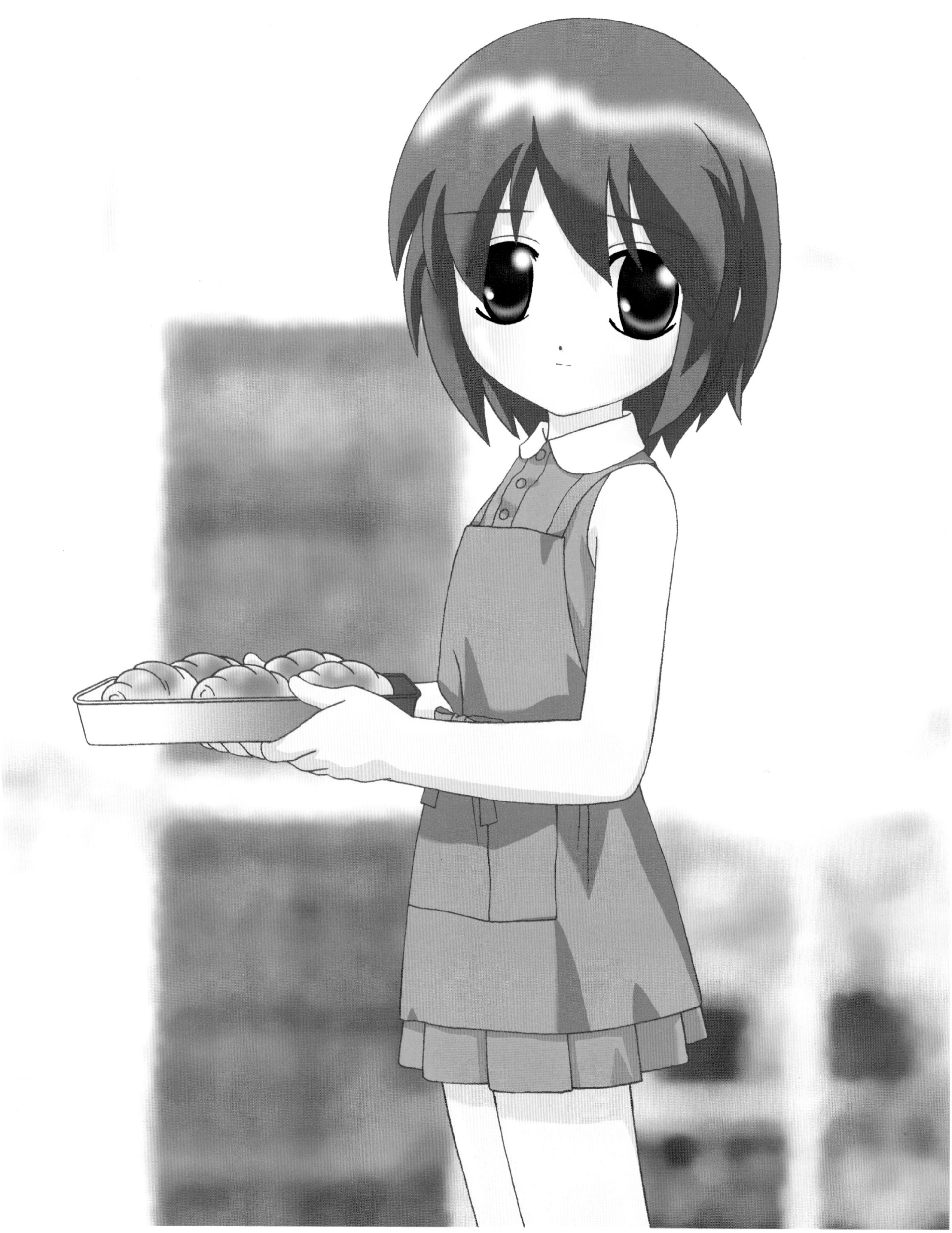

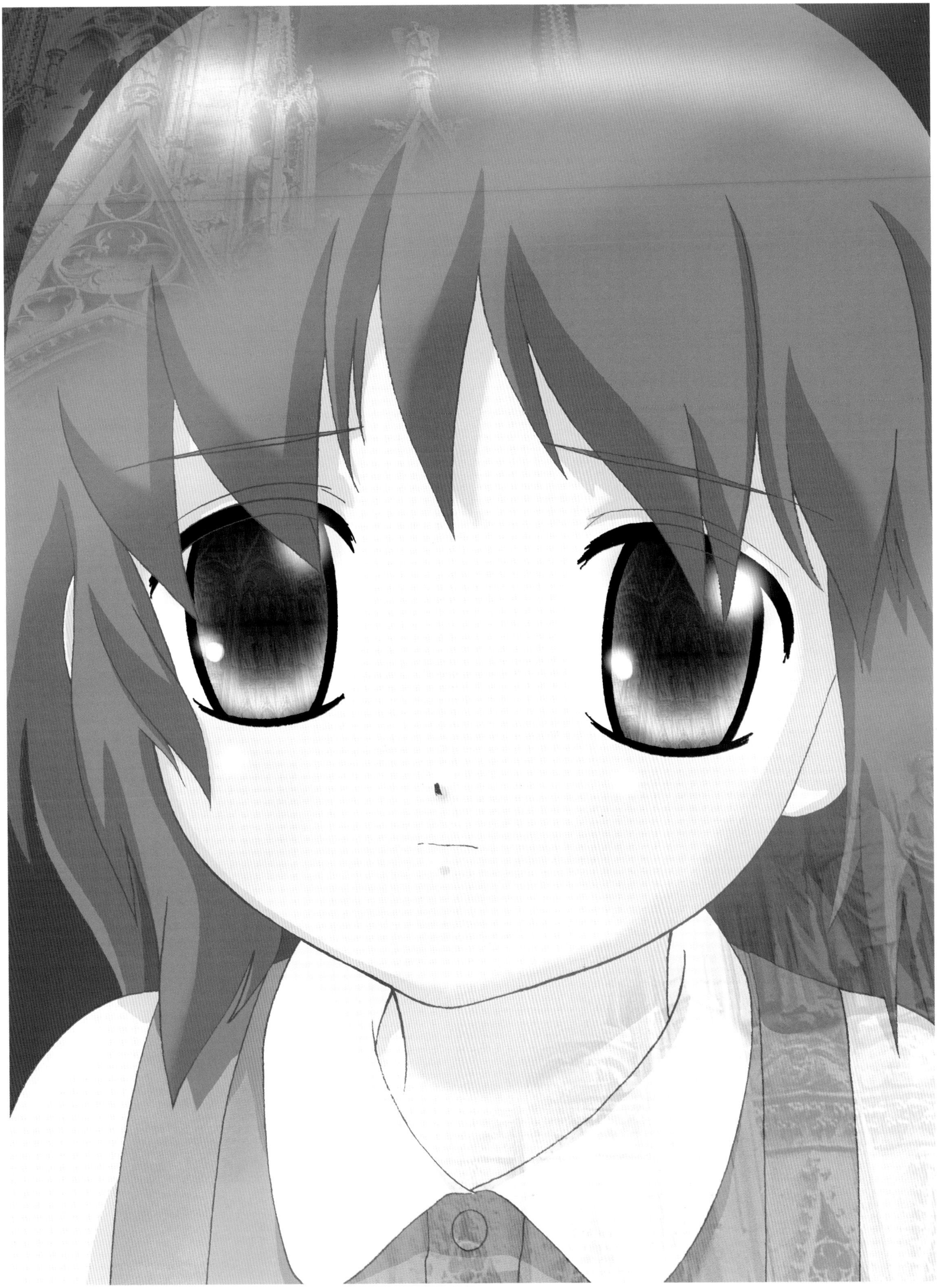

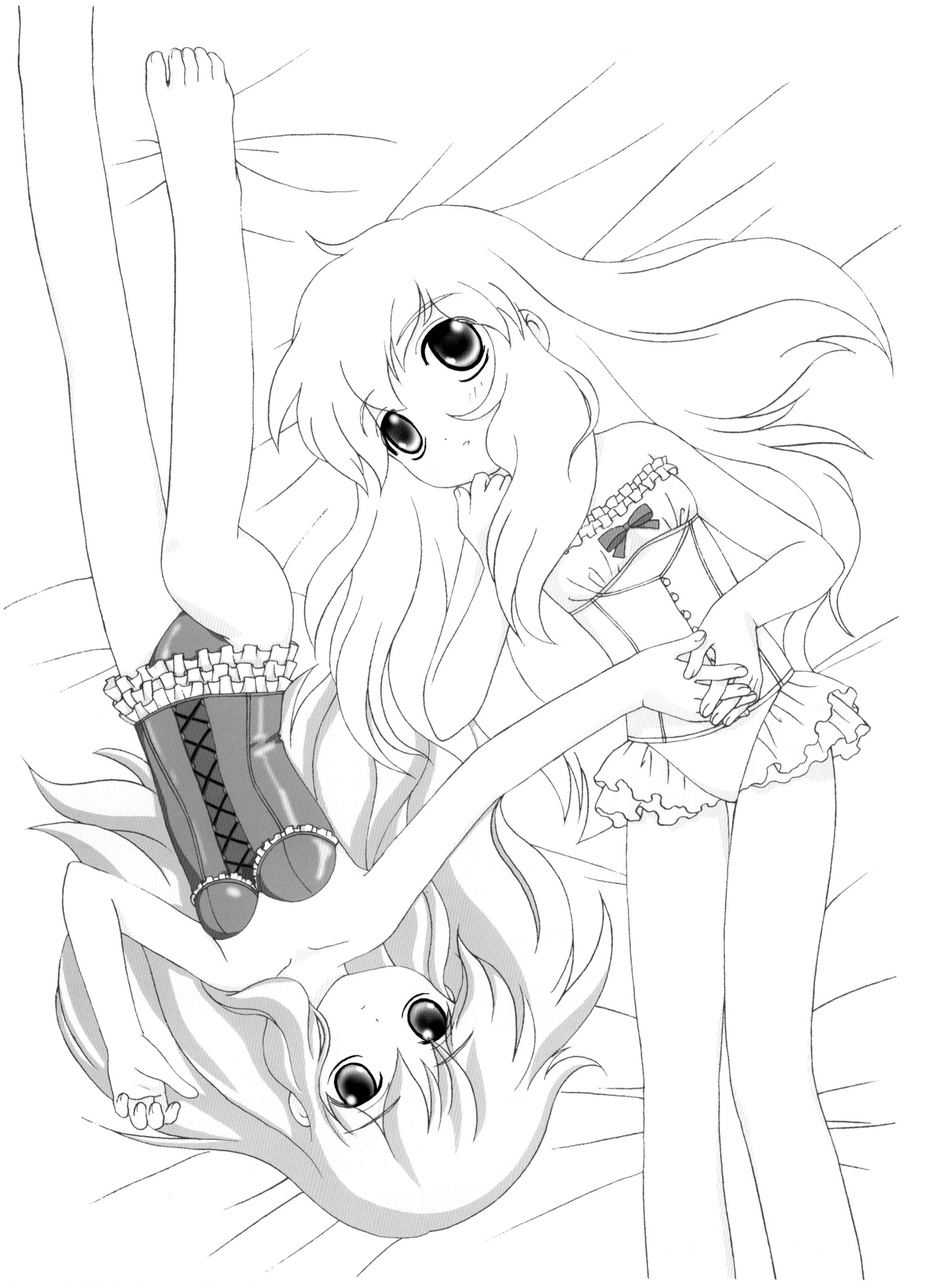

Kanako Sawada

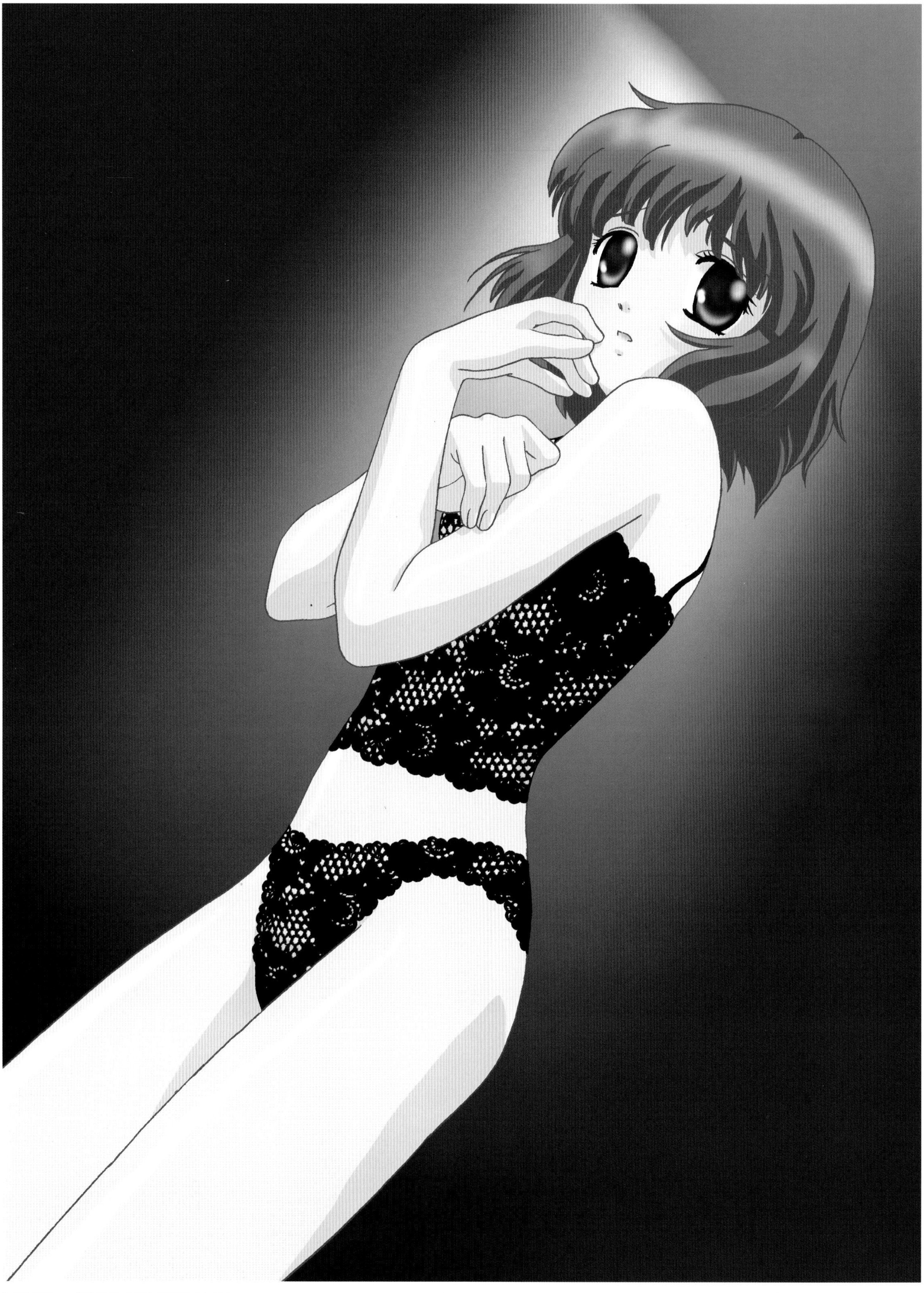

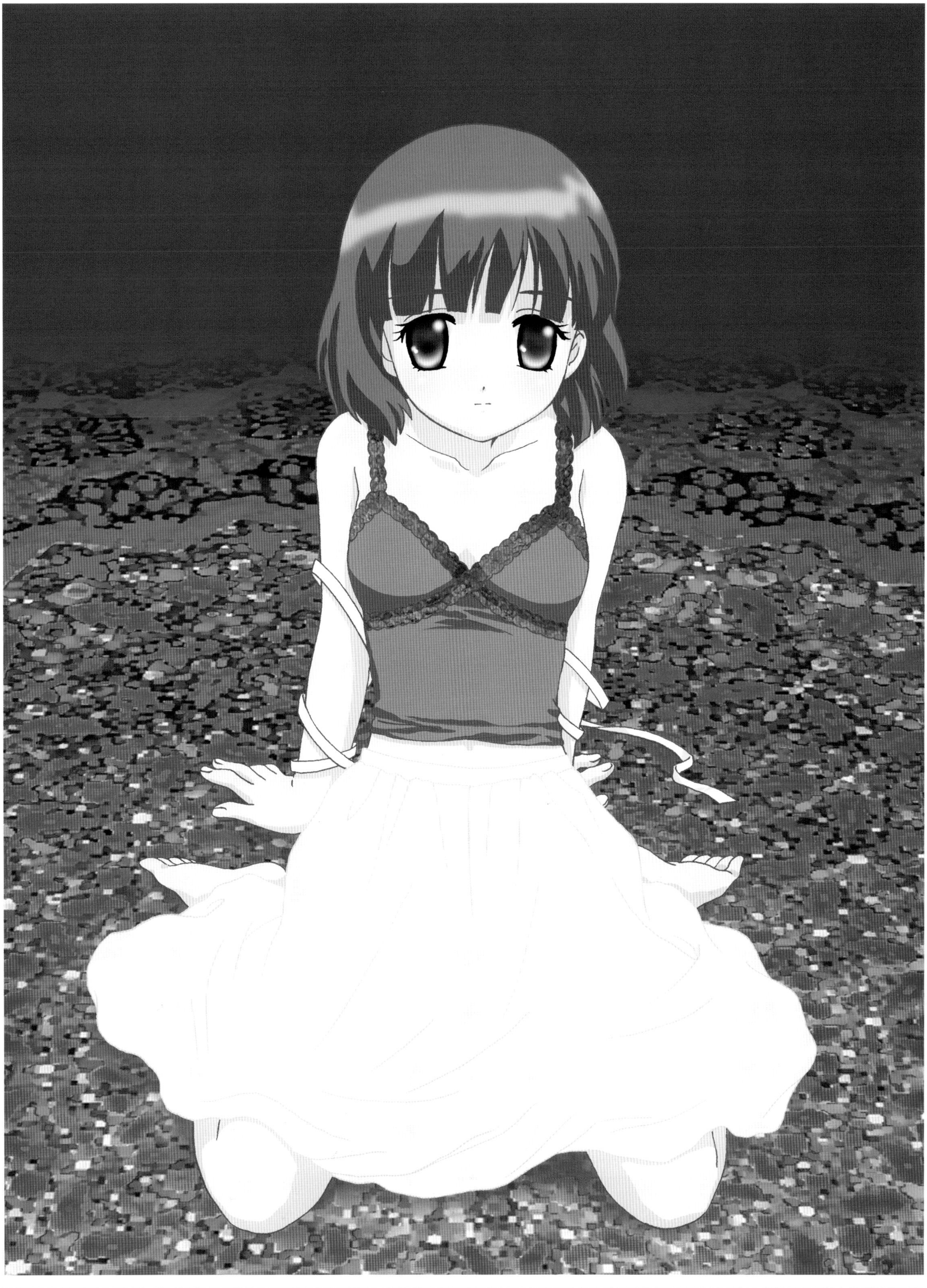

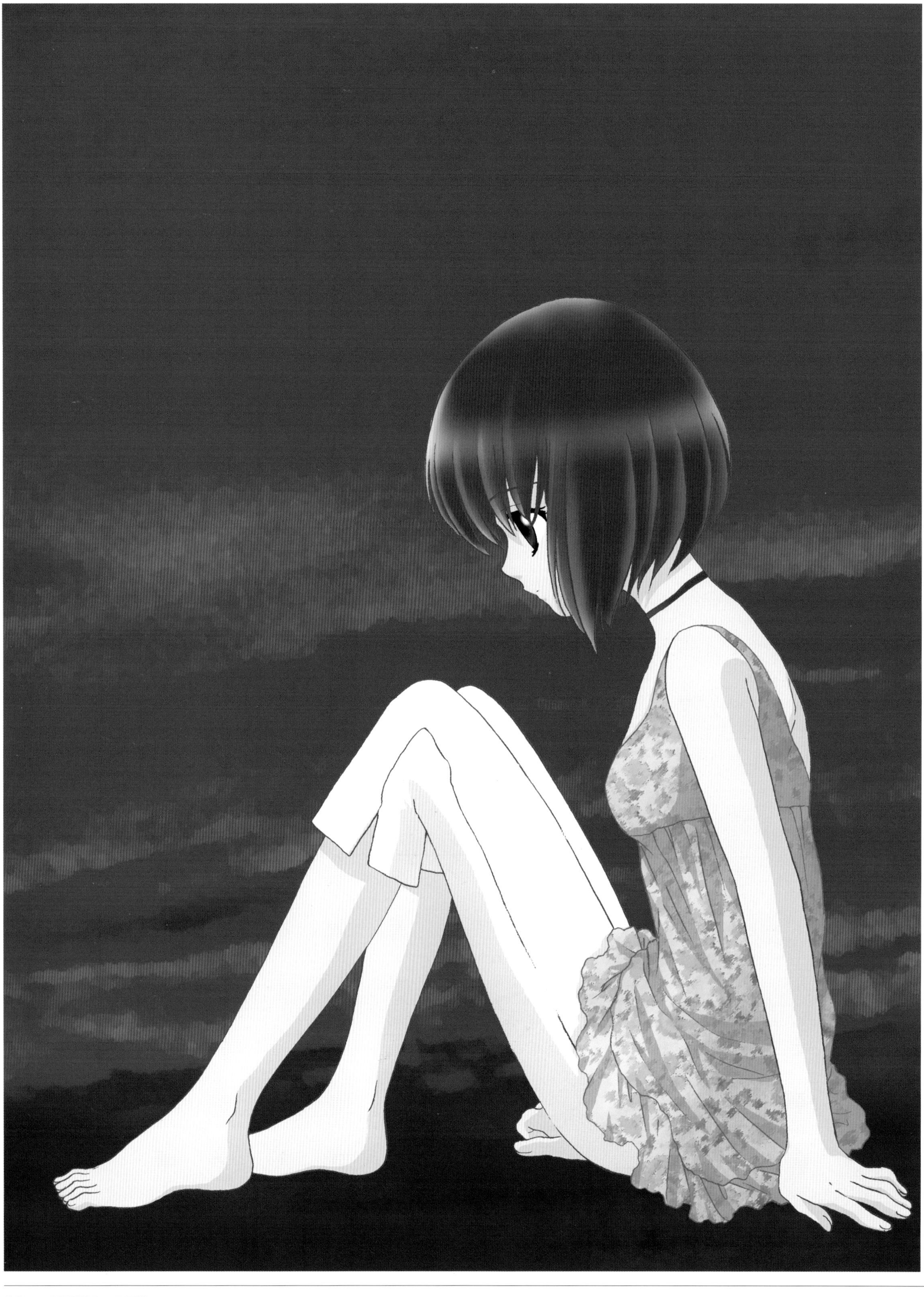

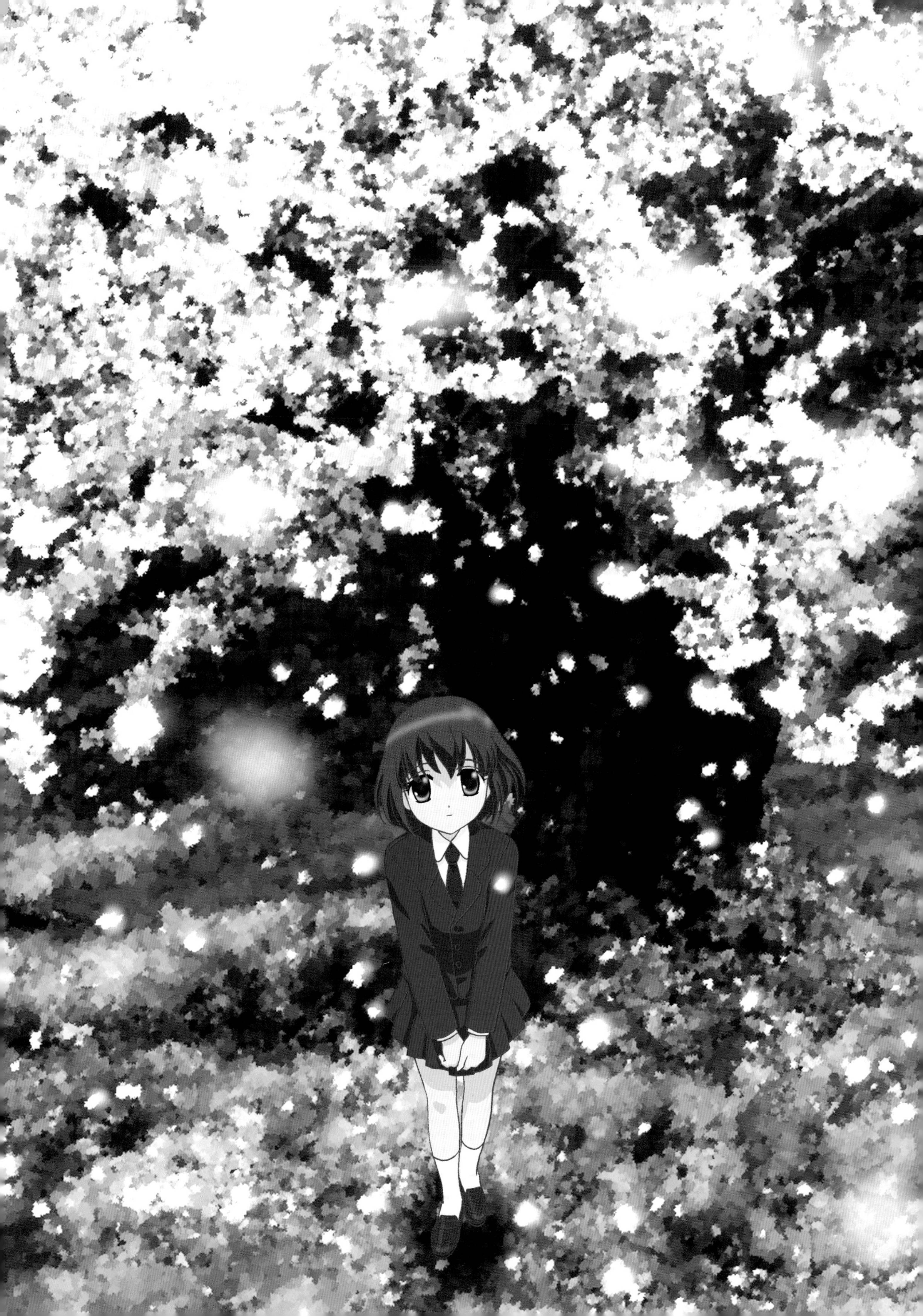

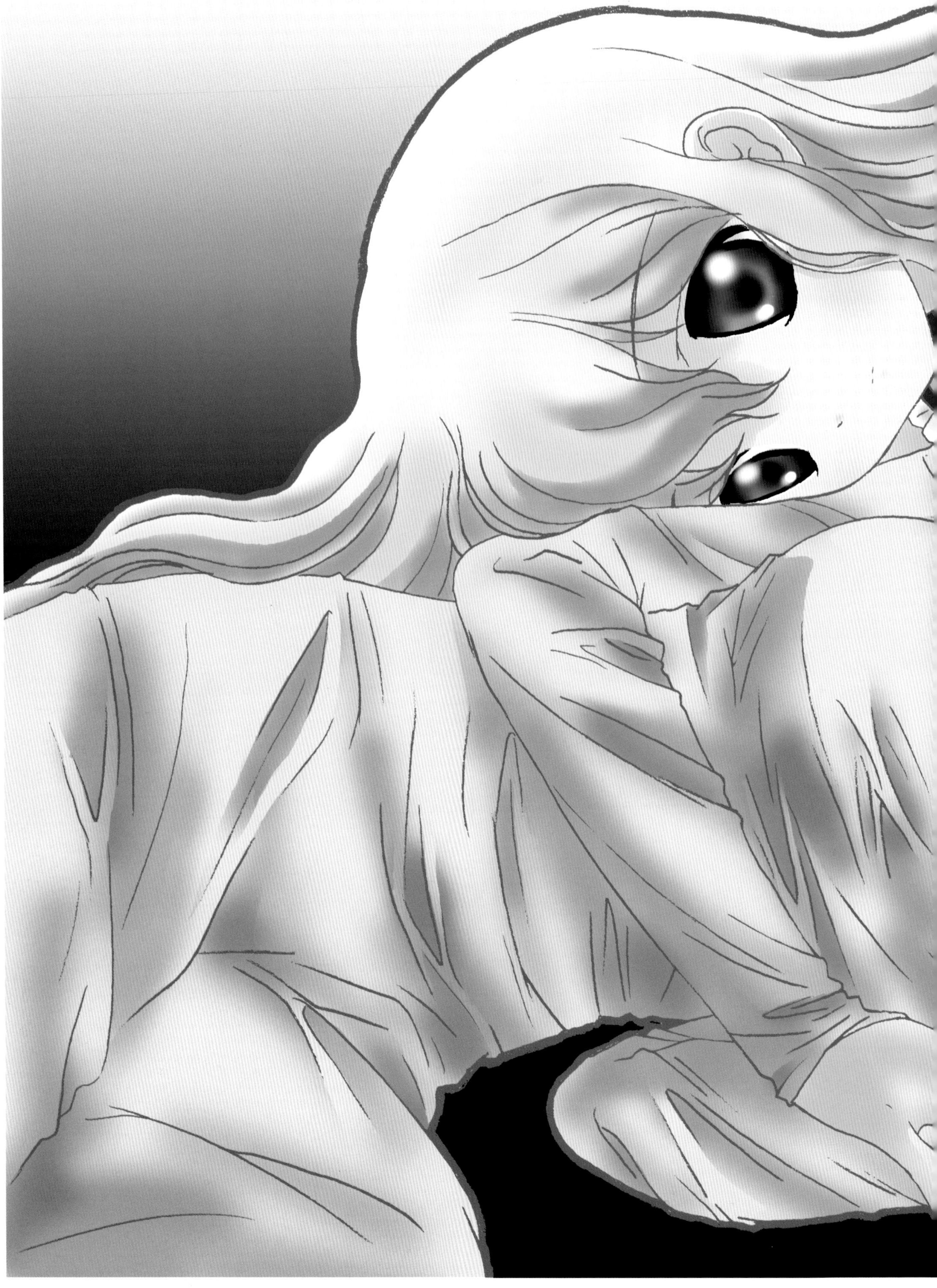

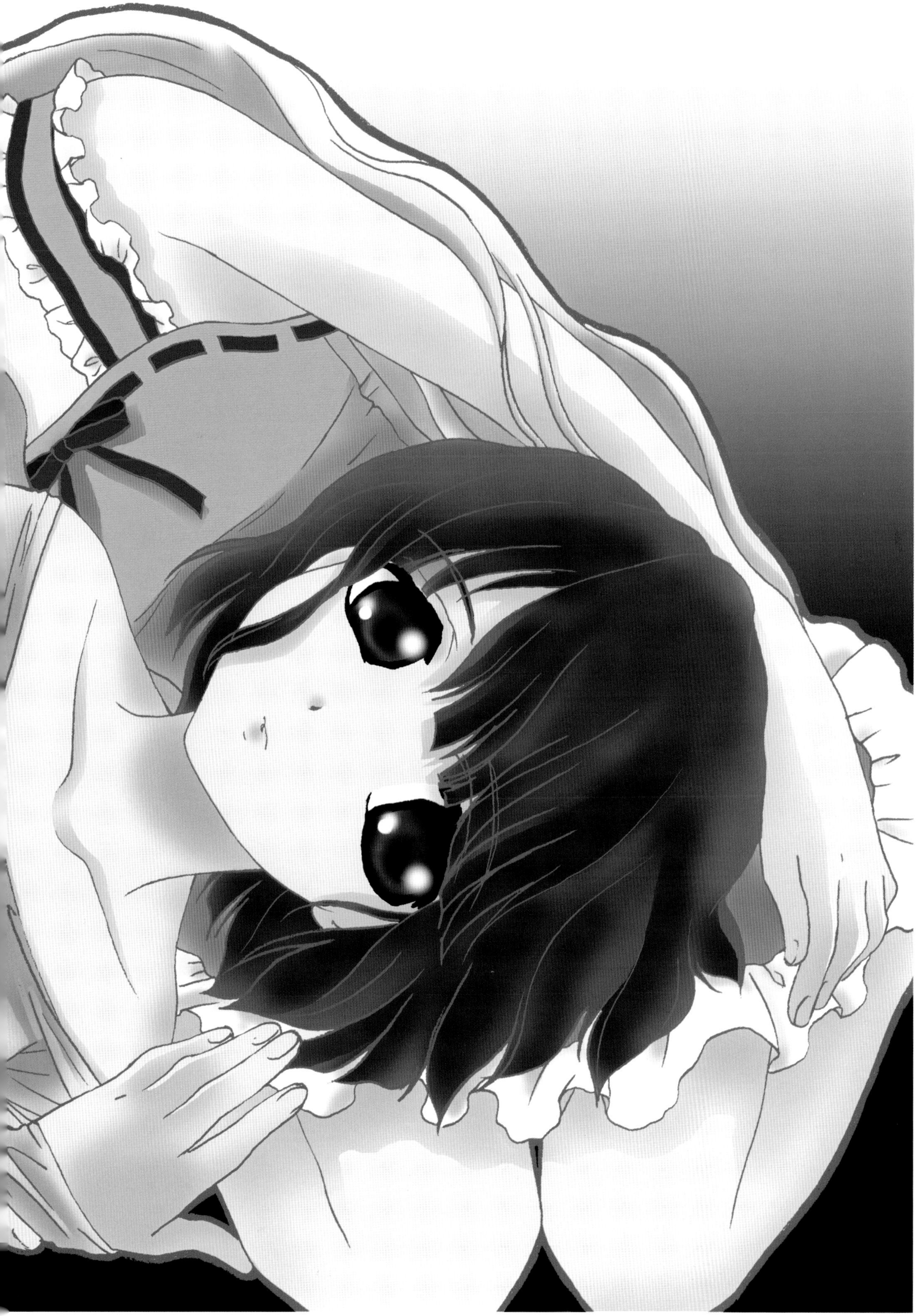

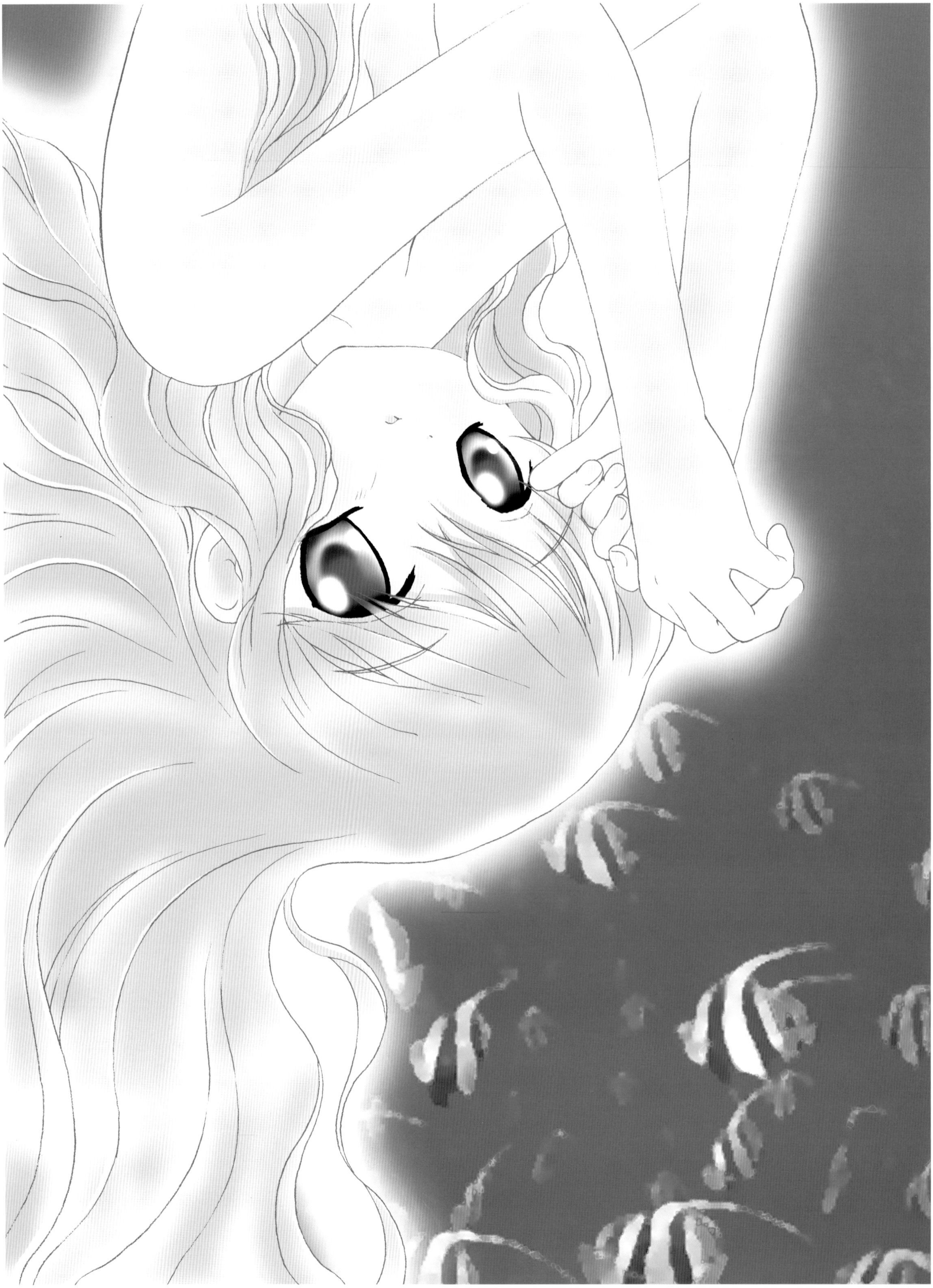

Ryo Hayama

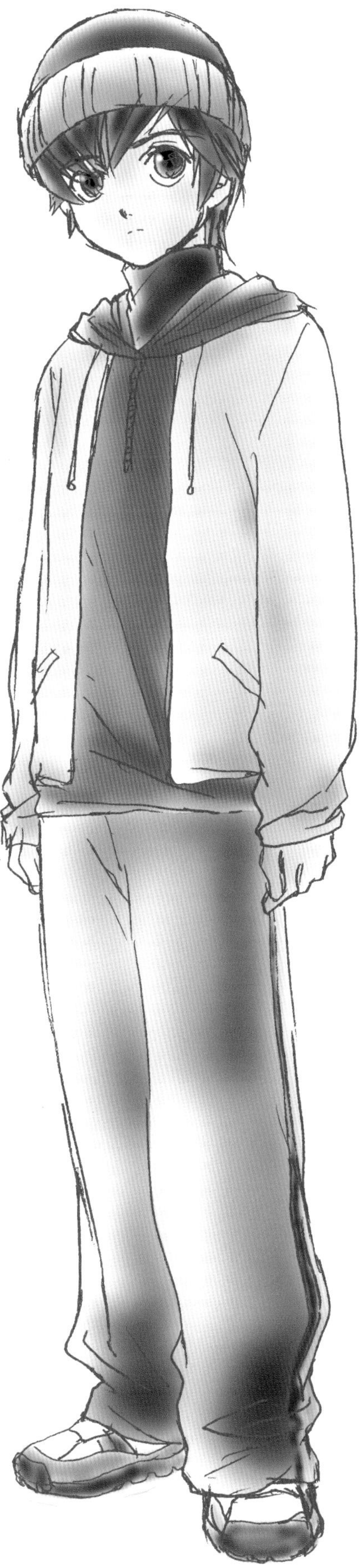

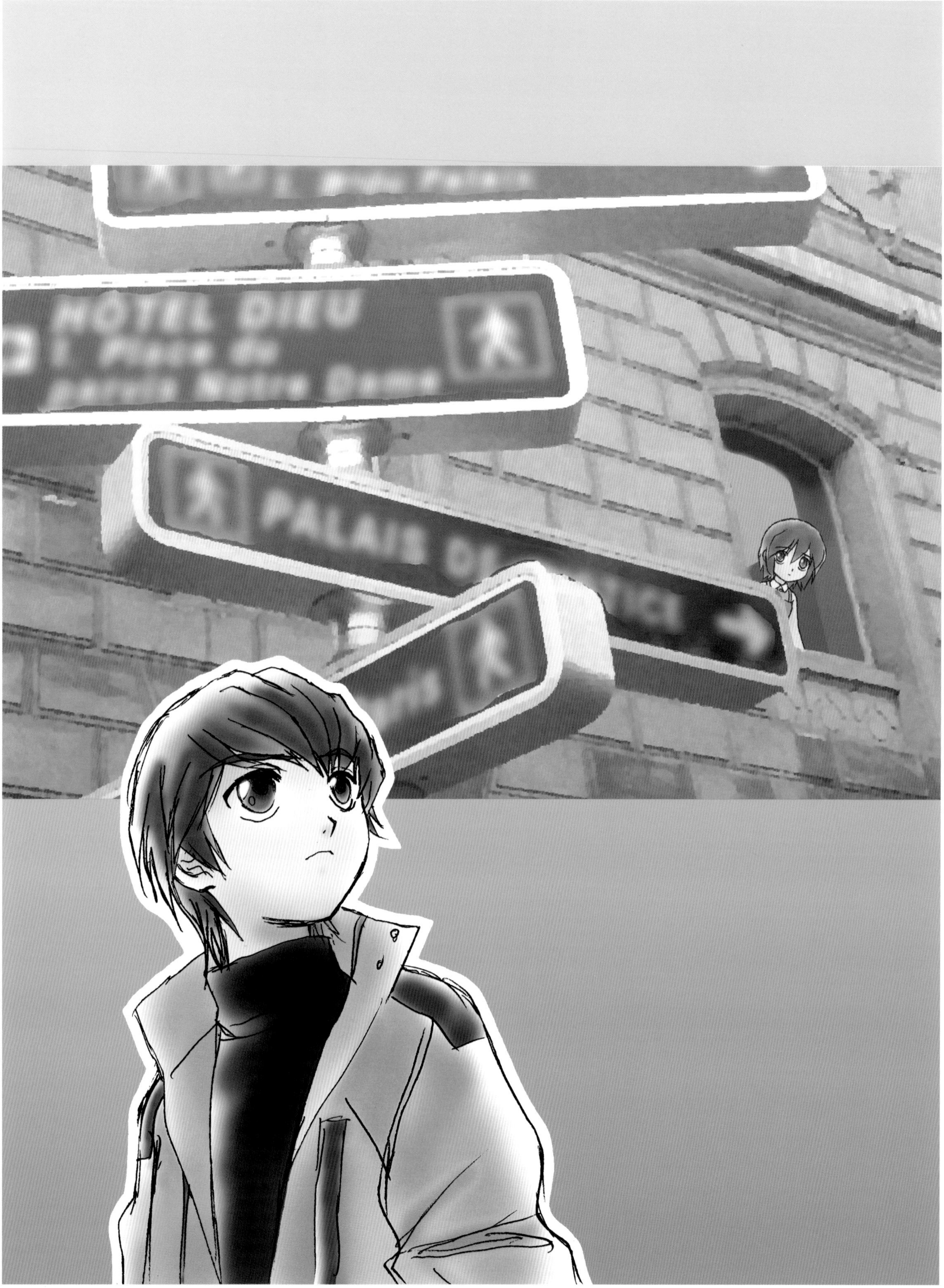
HÔTEL DIEU
1 Place du
PALAIS

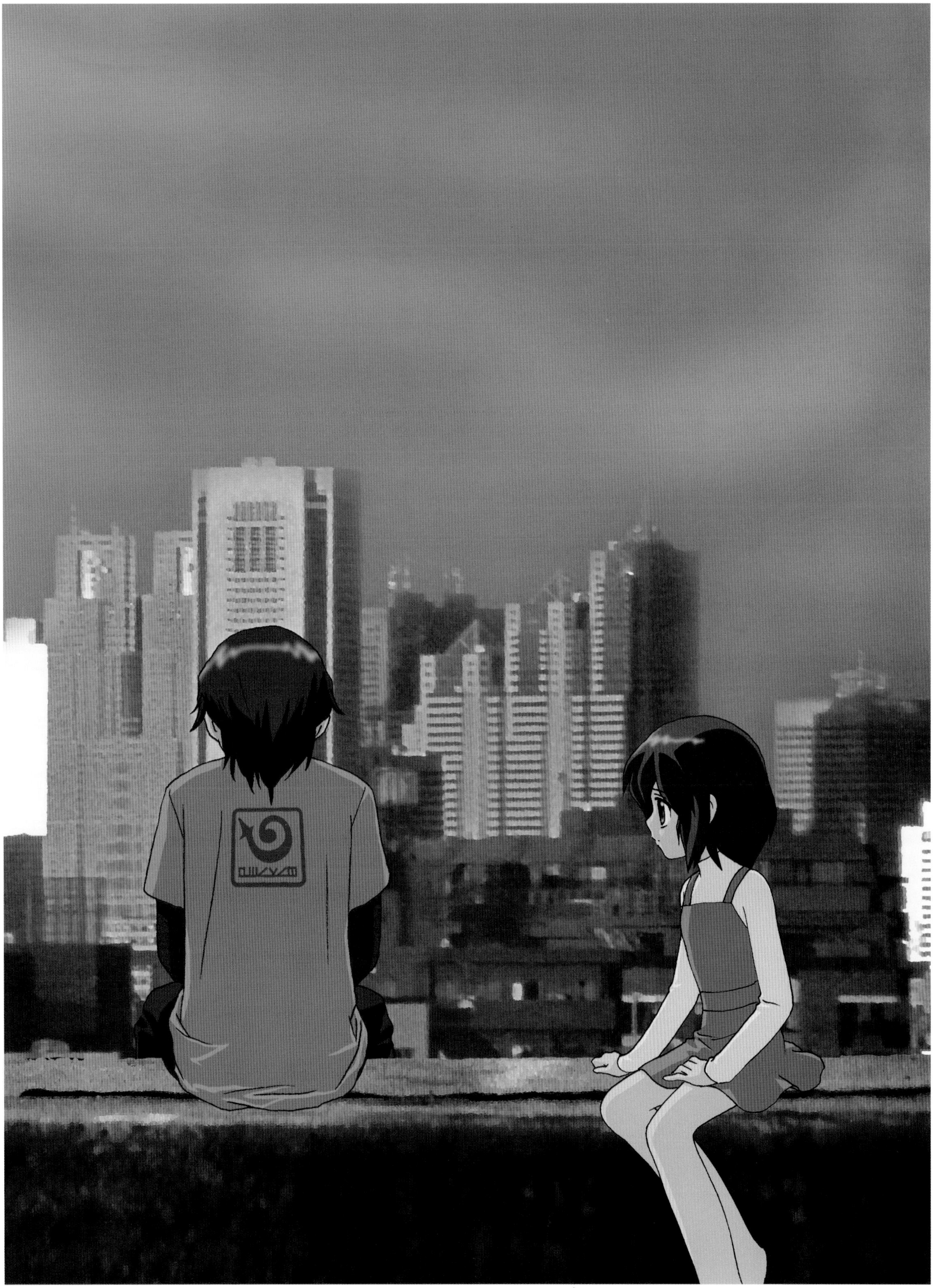

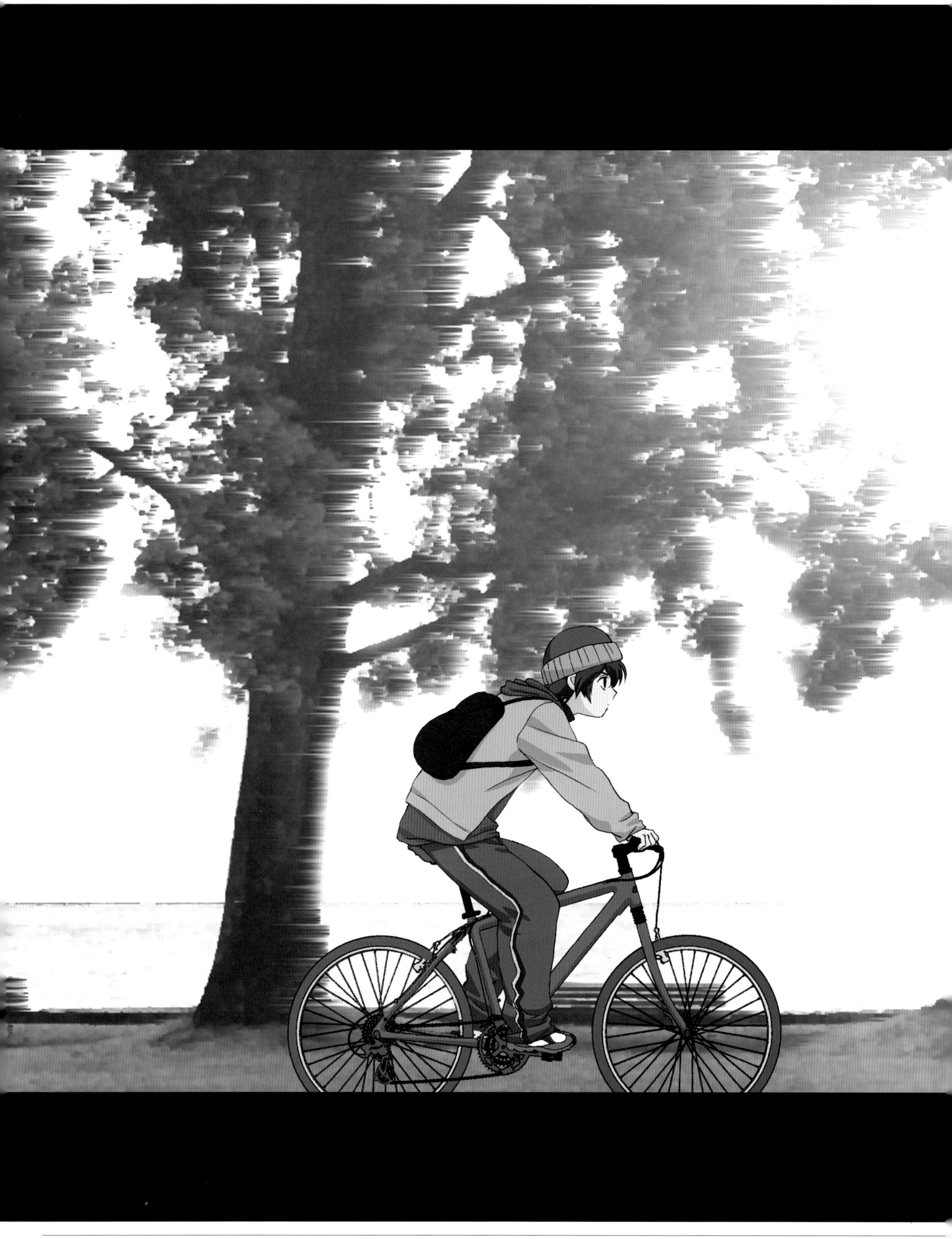

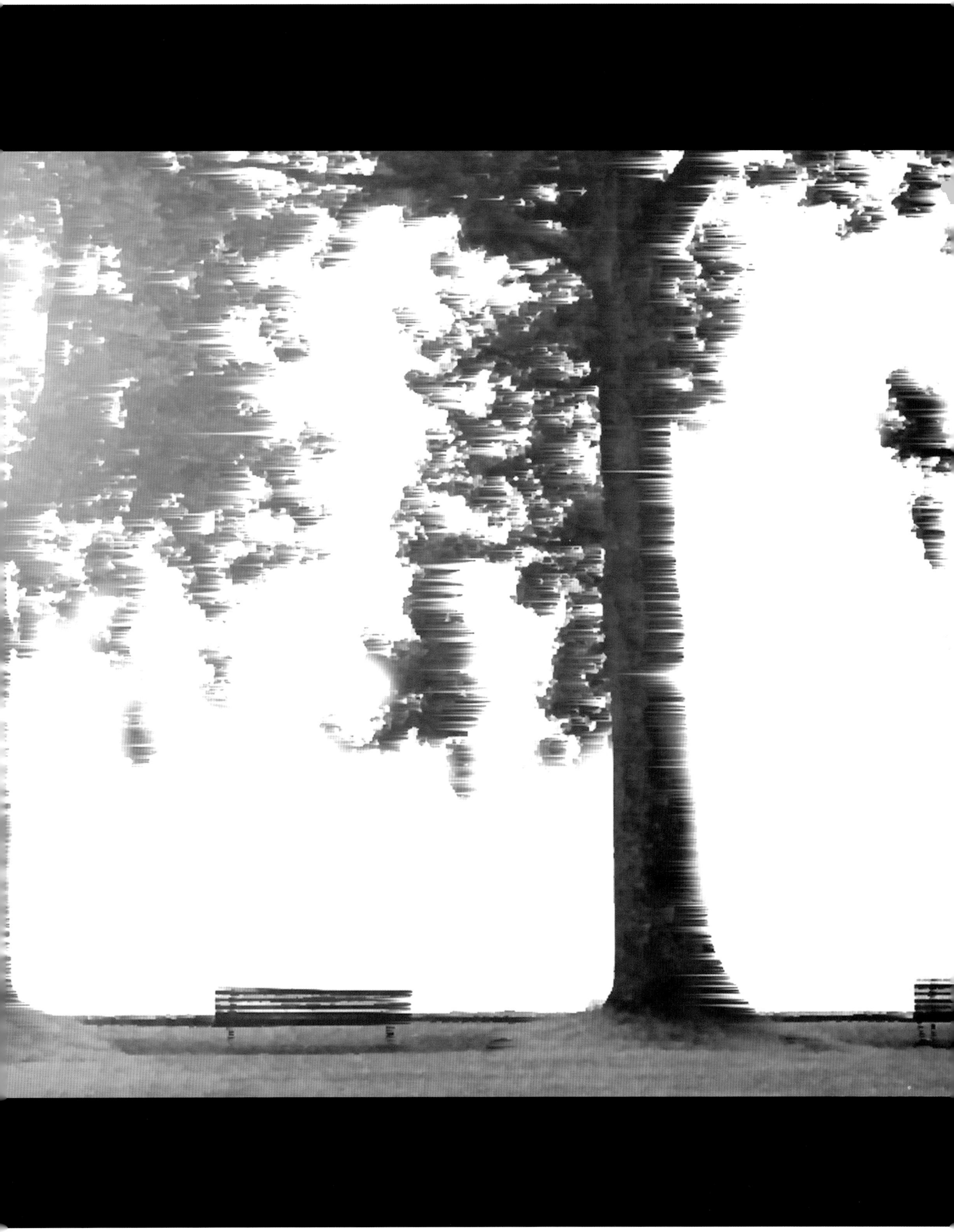

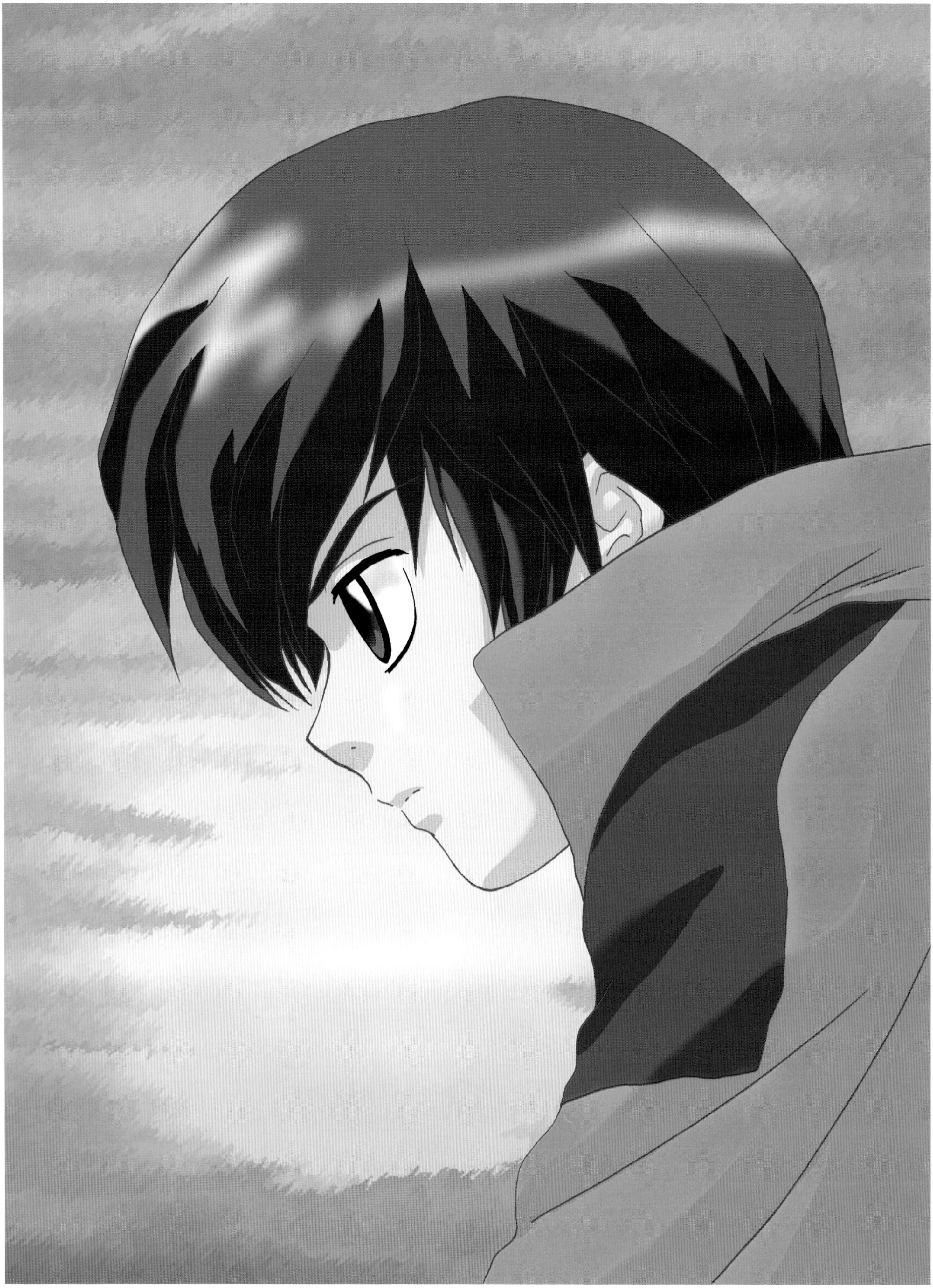

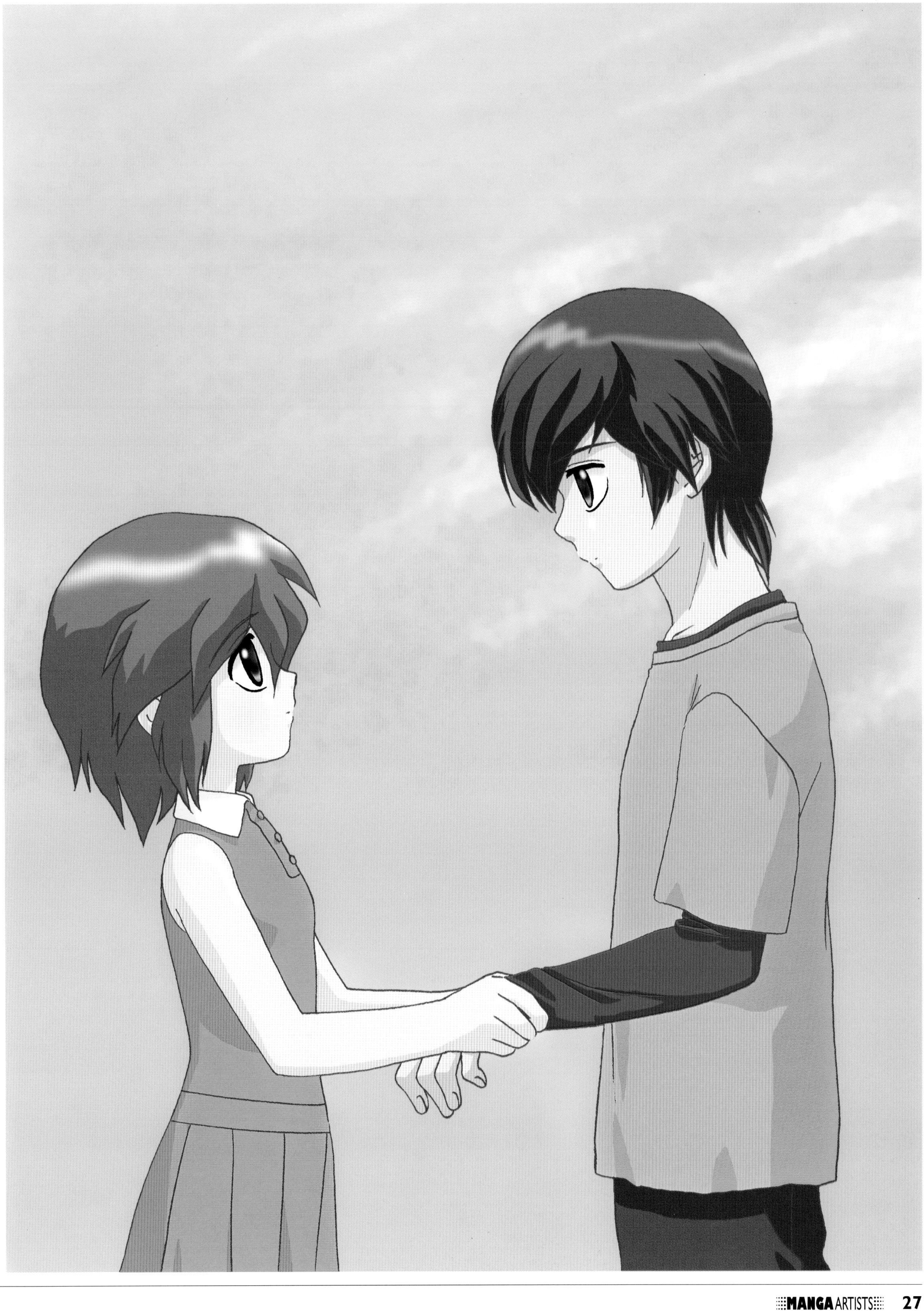

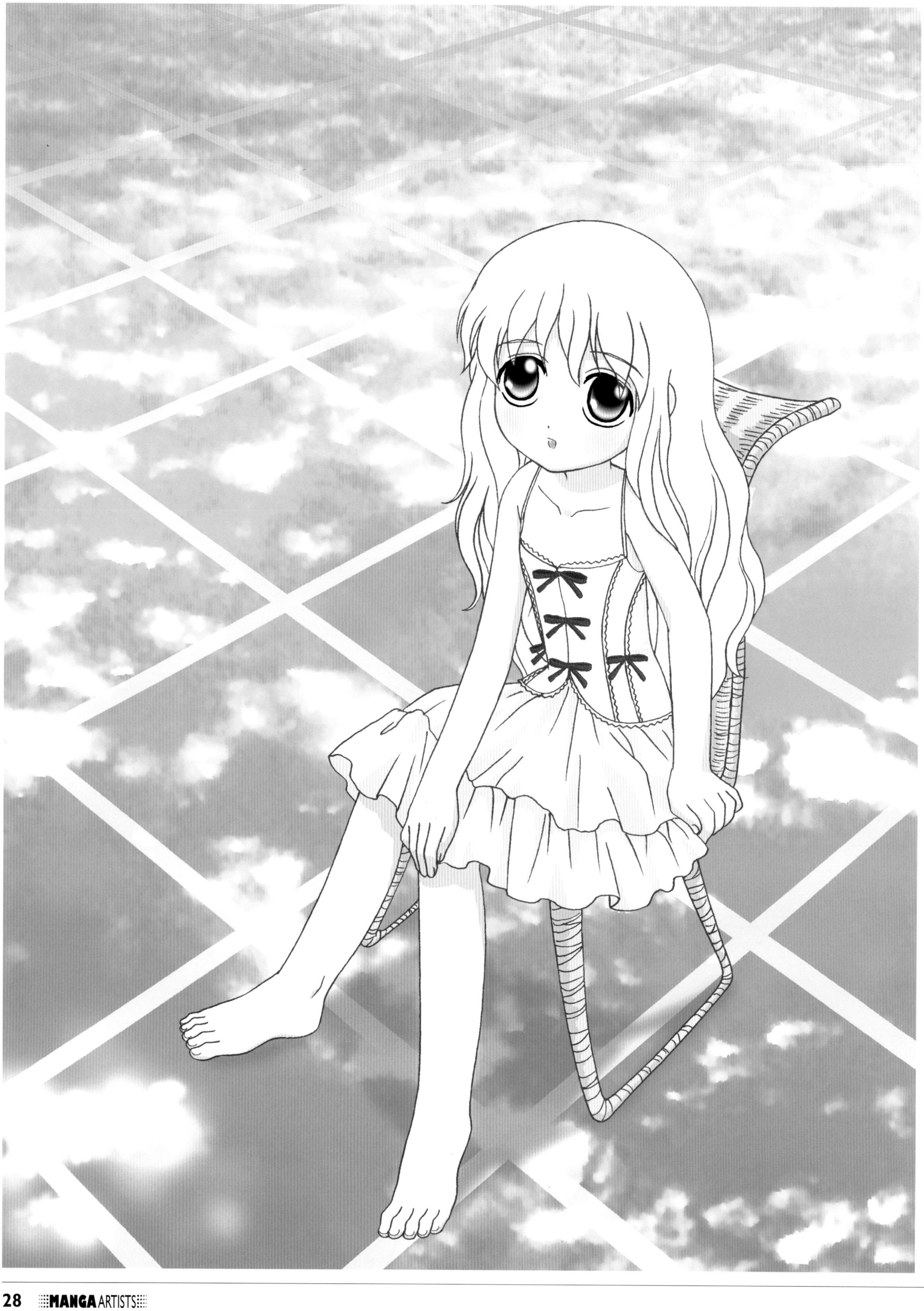

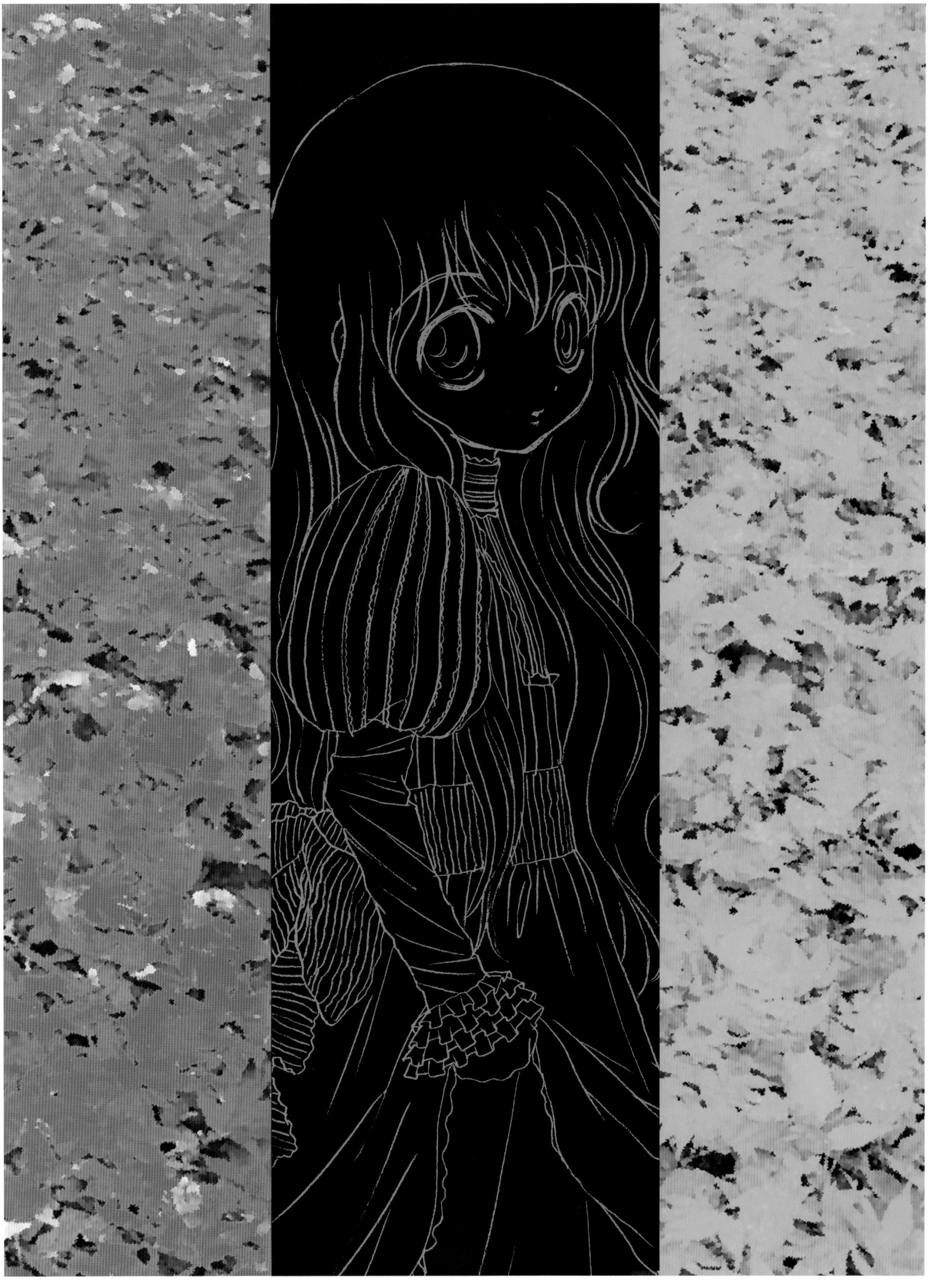

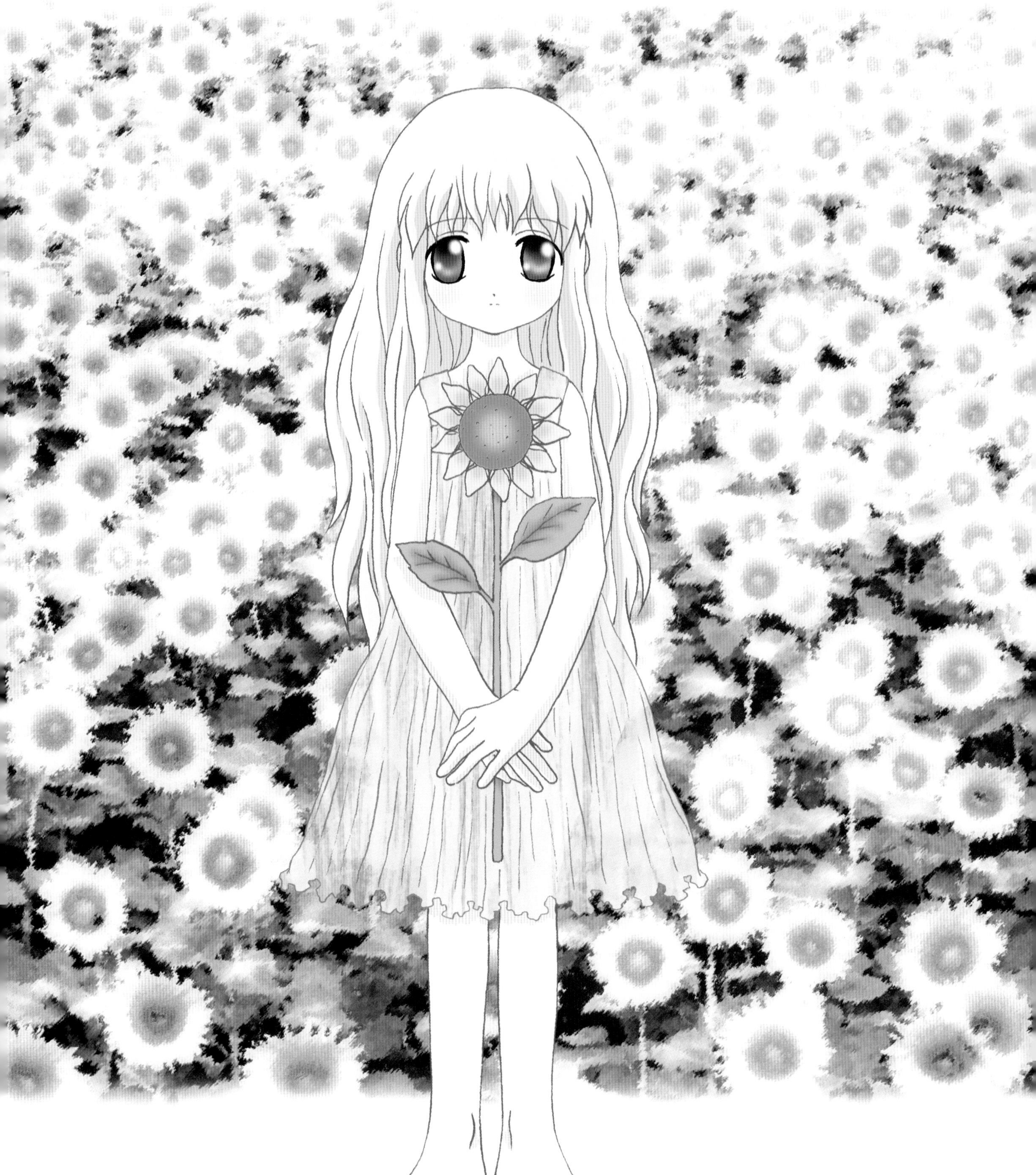

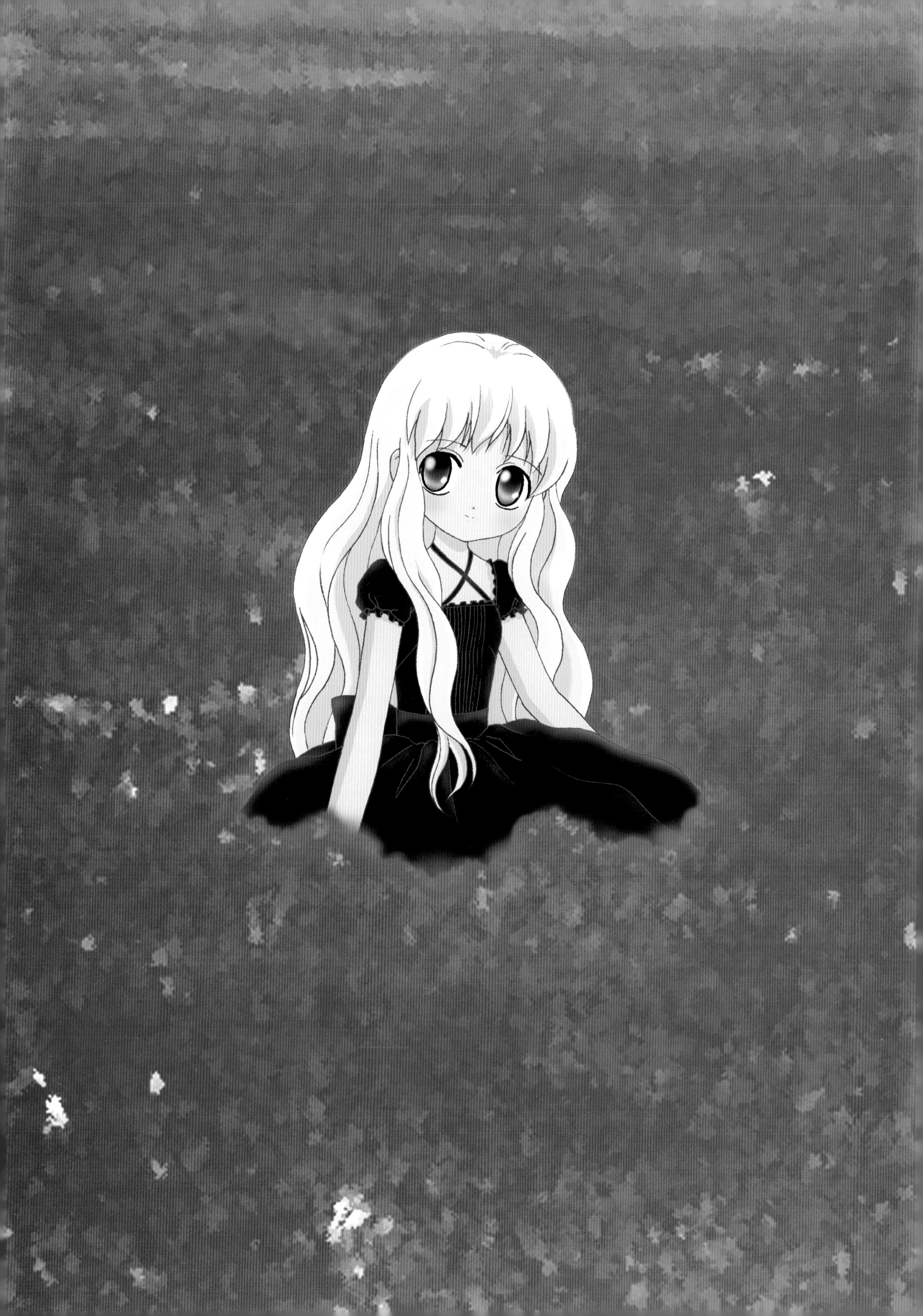

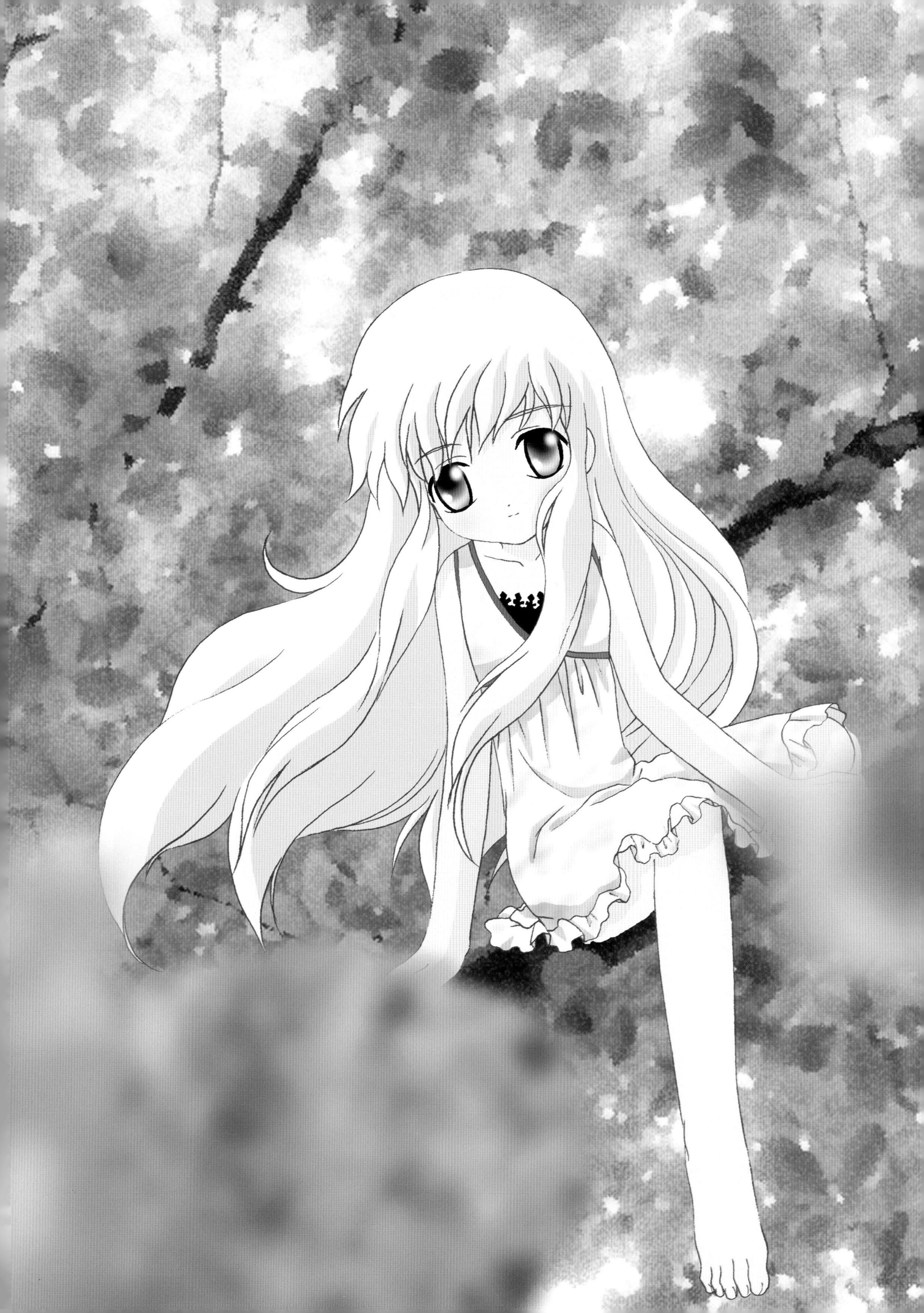

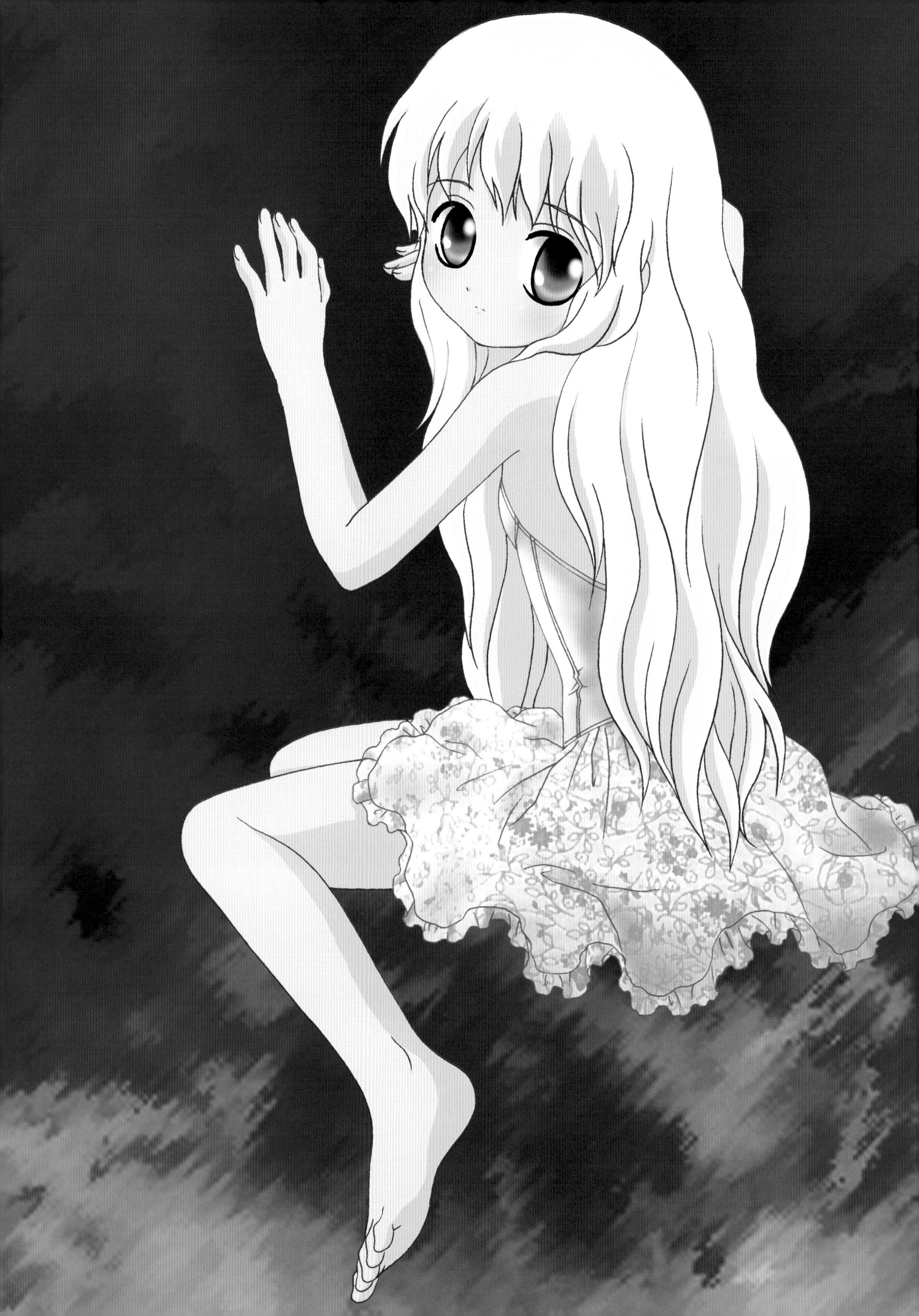

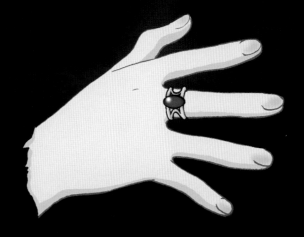

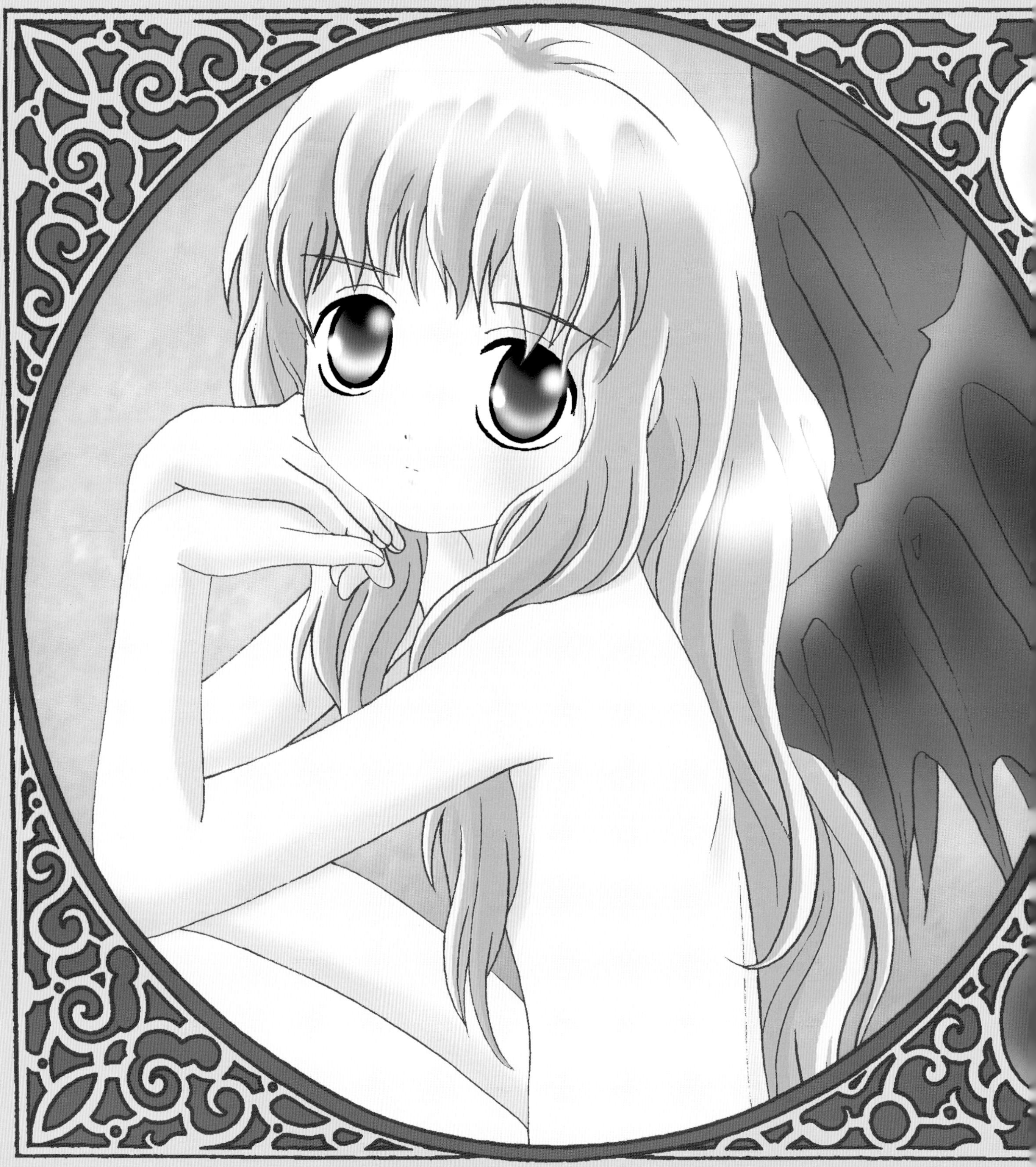

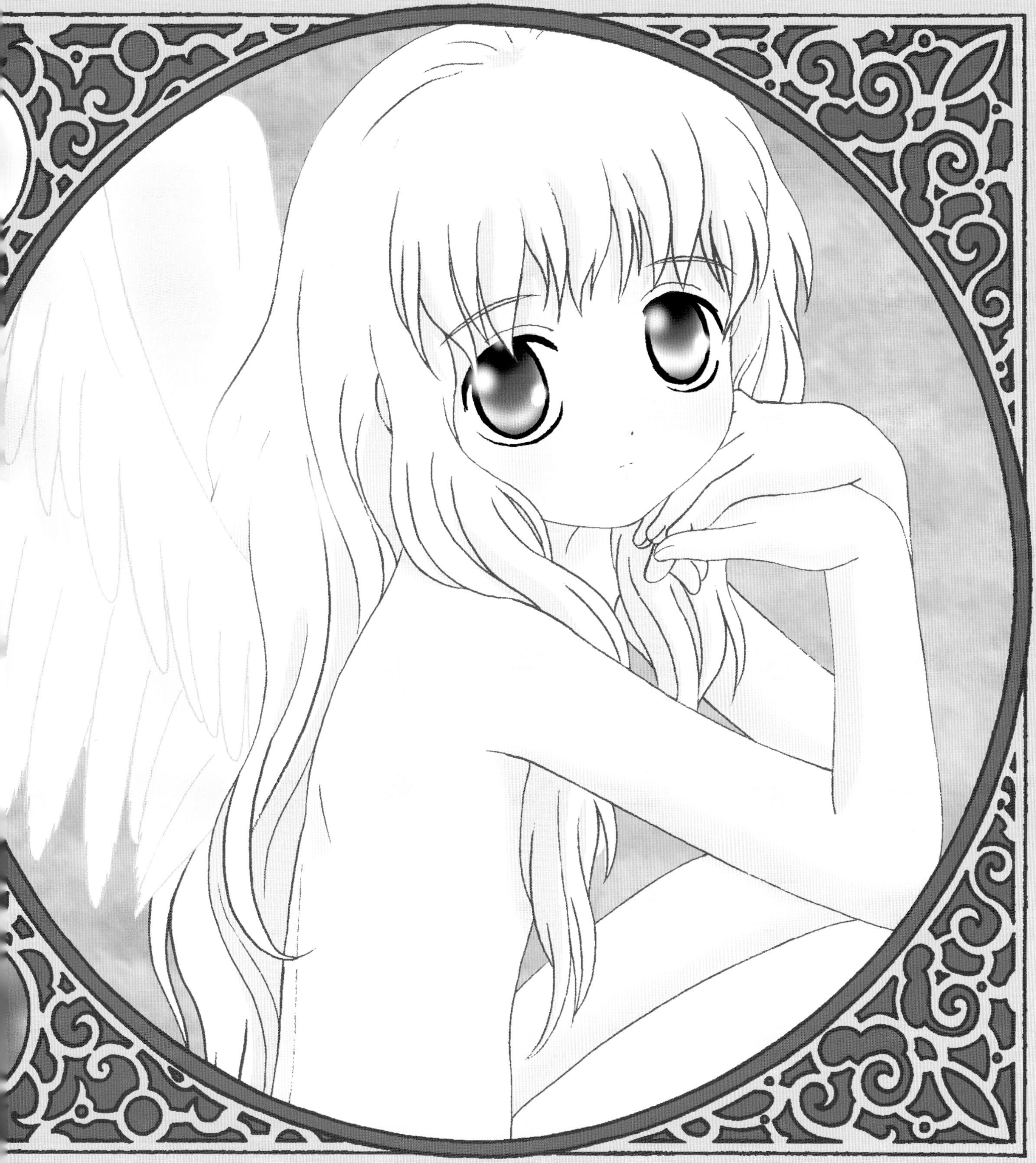

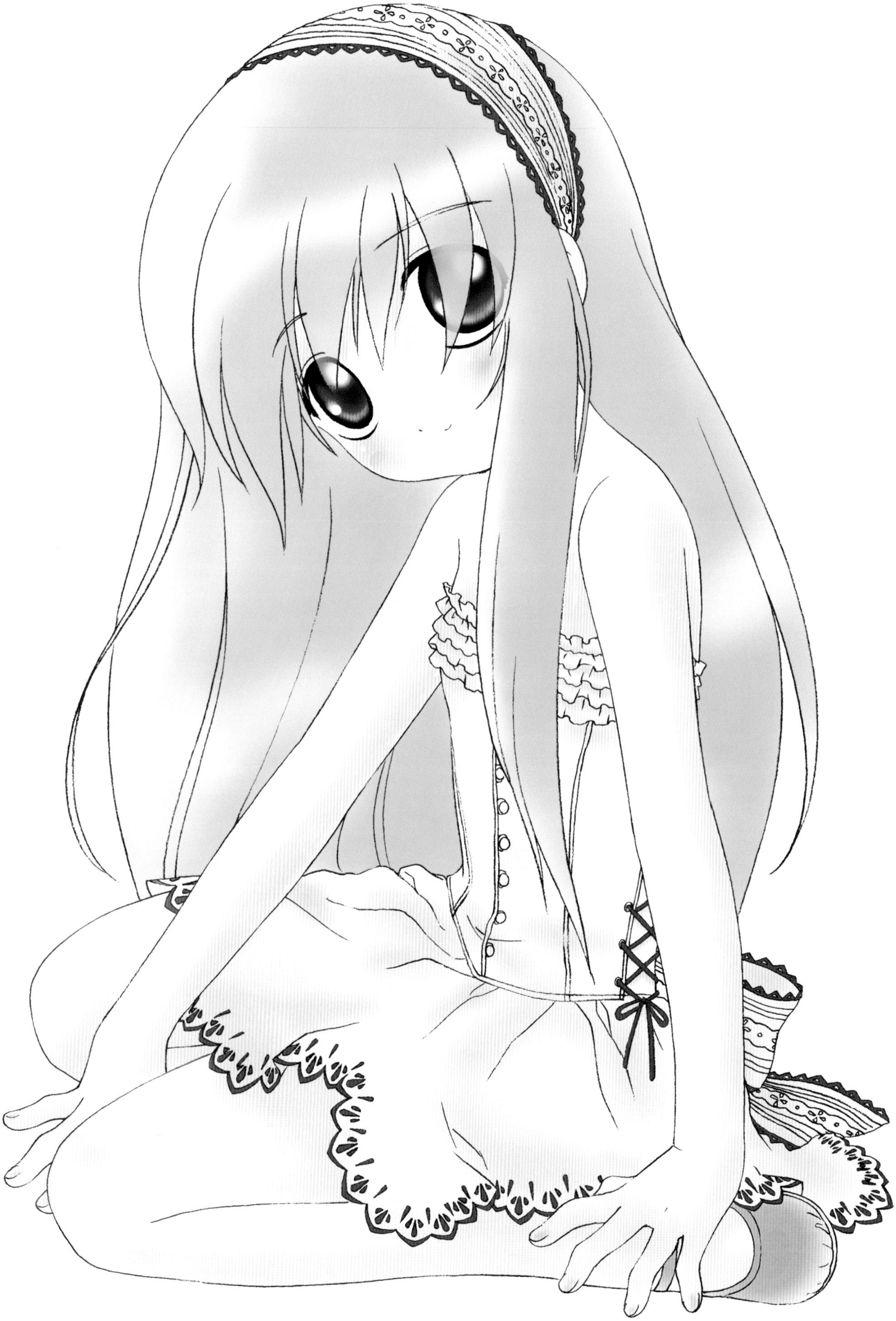

Alisa Nojima

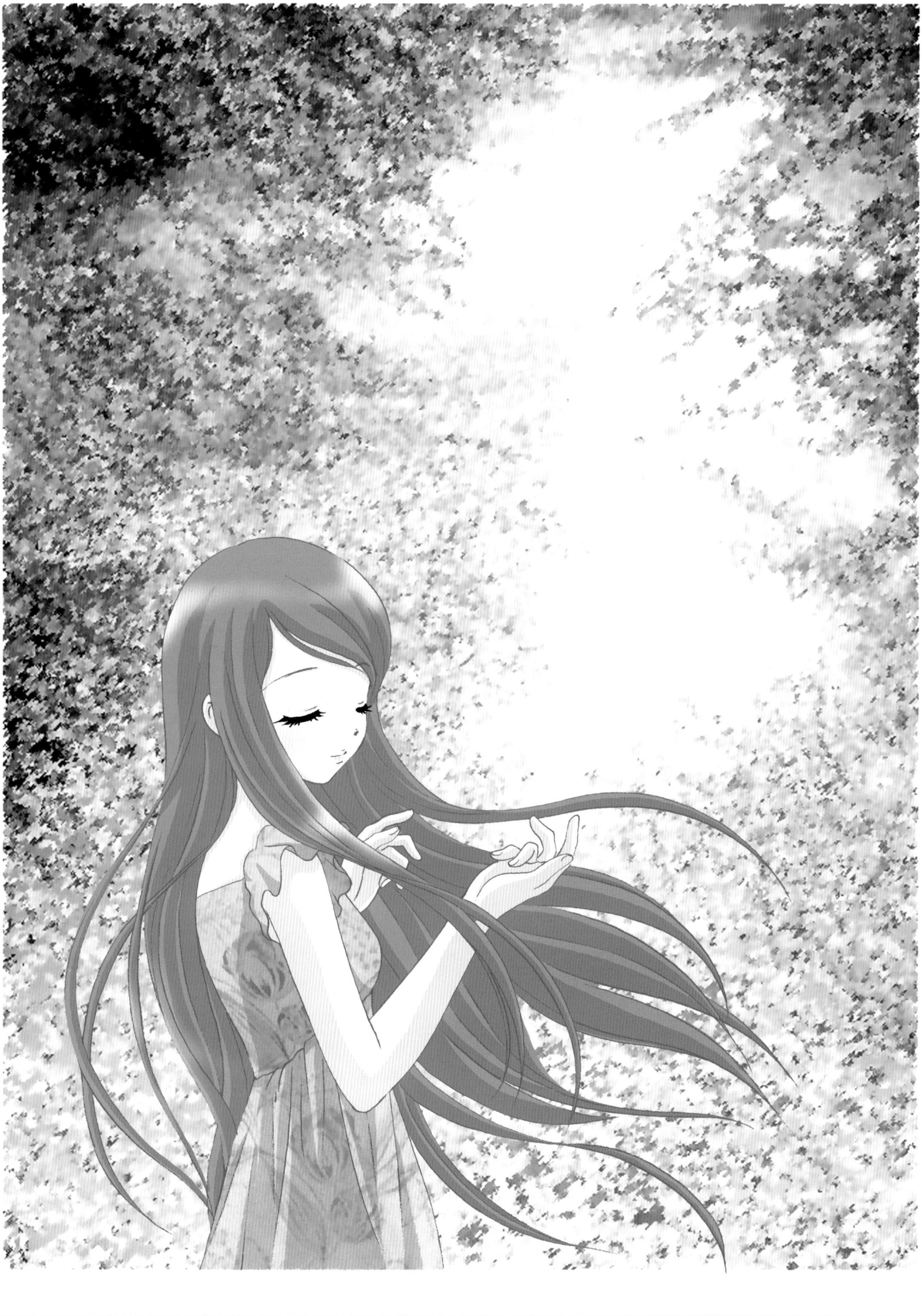

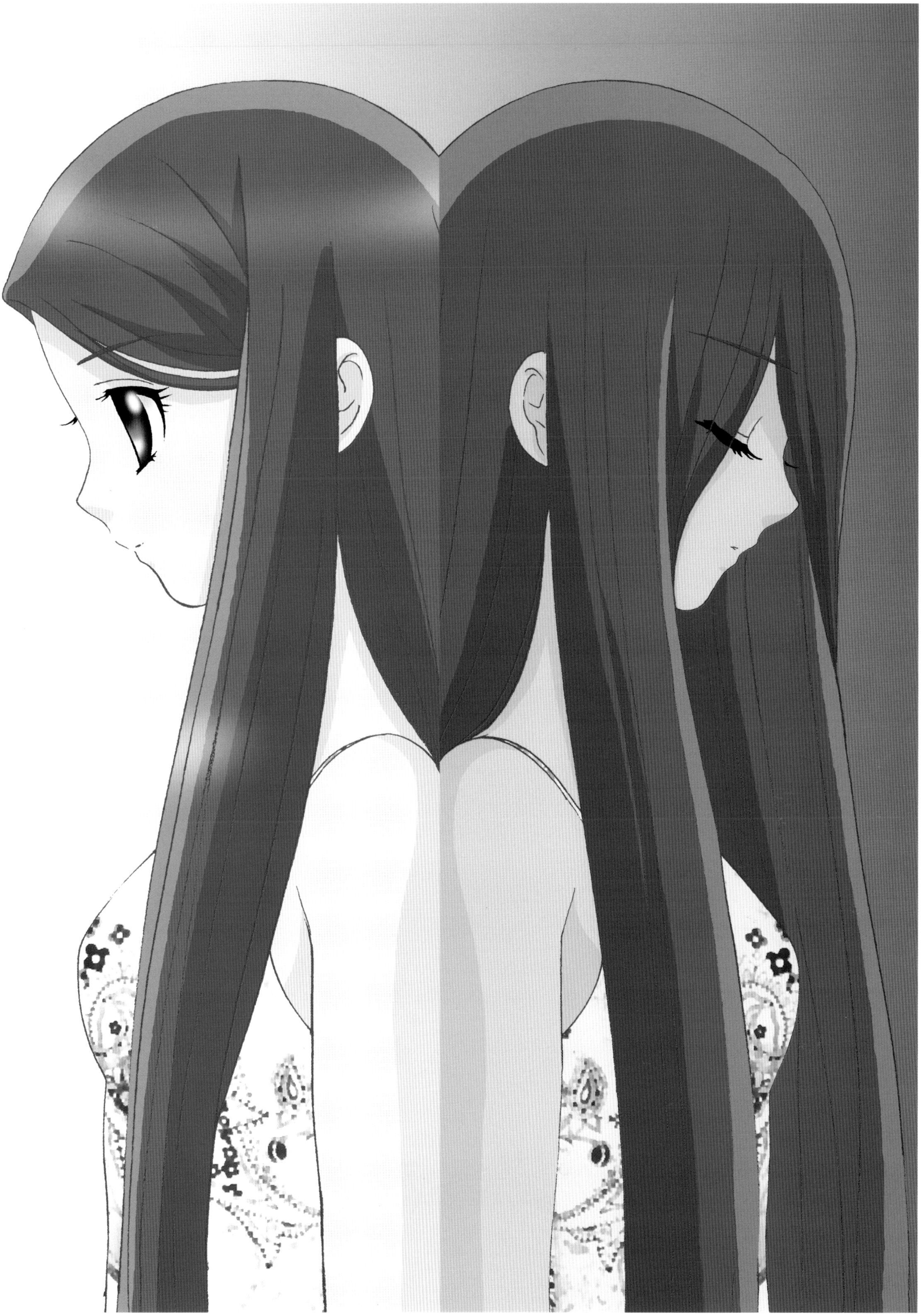

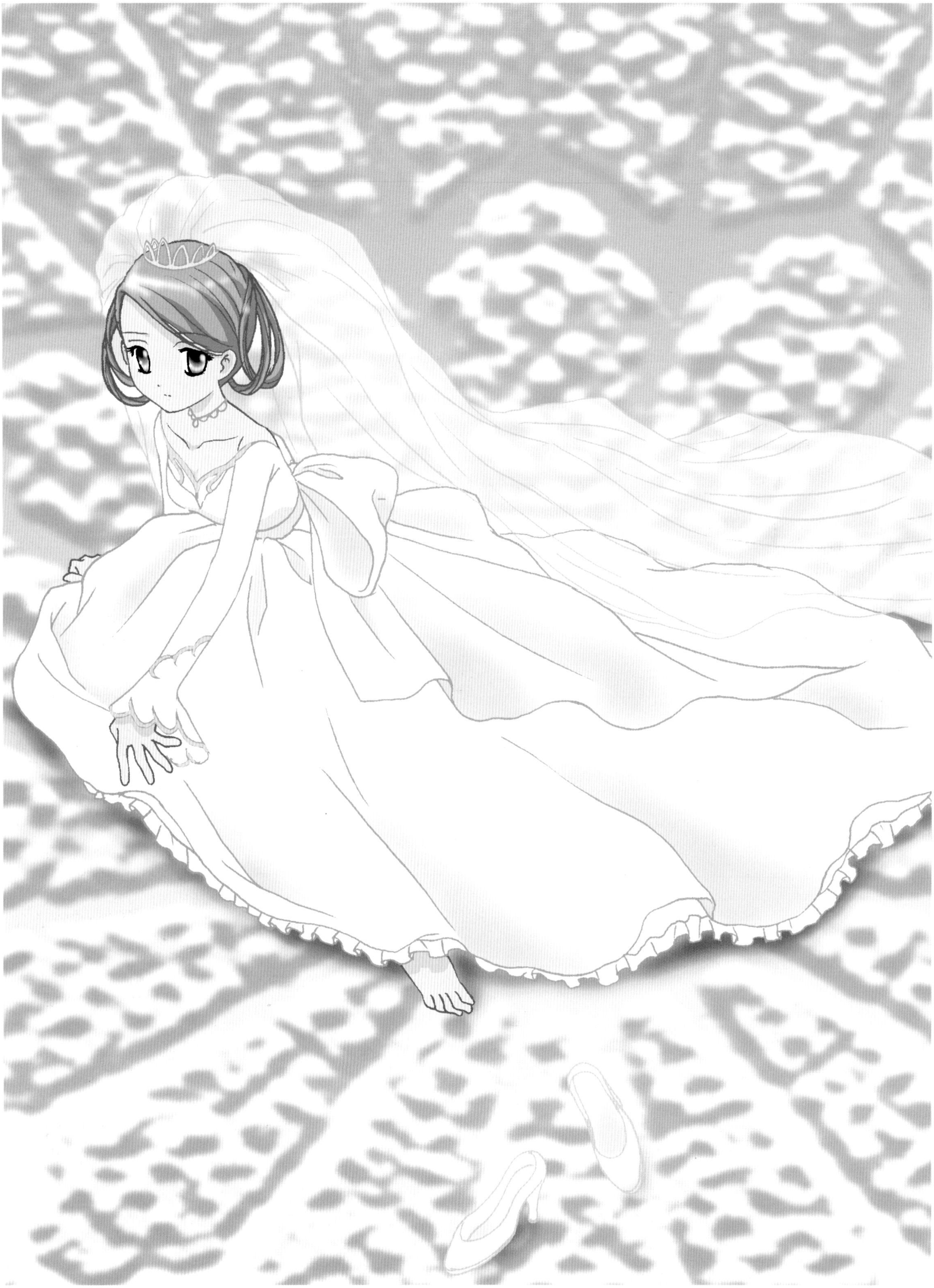

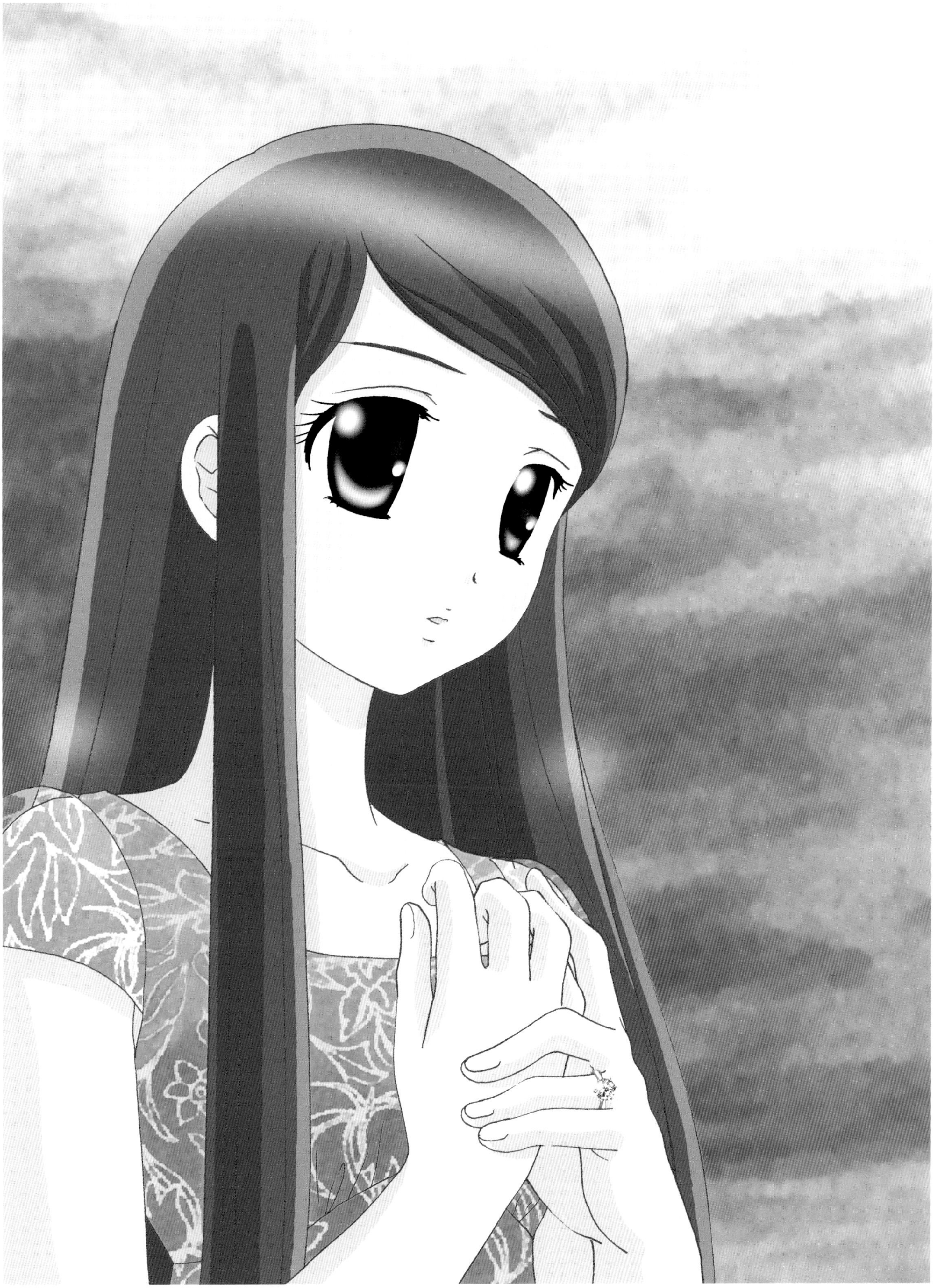

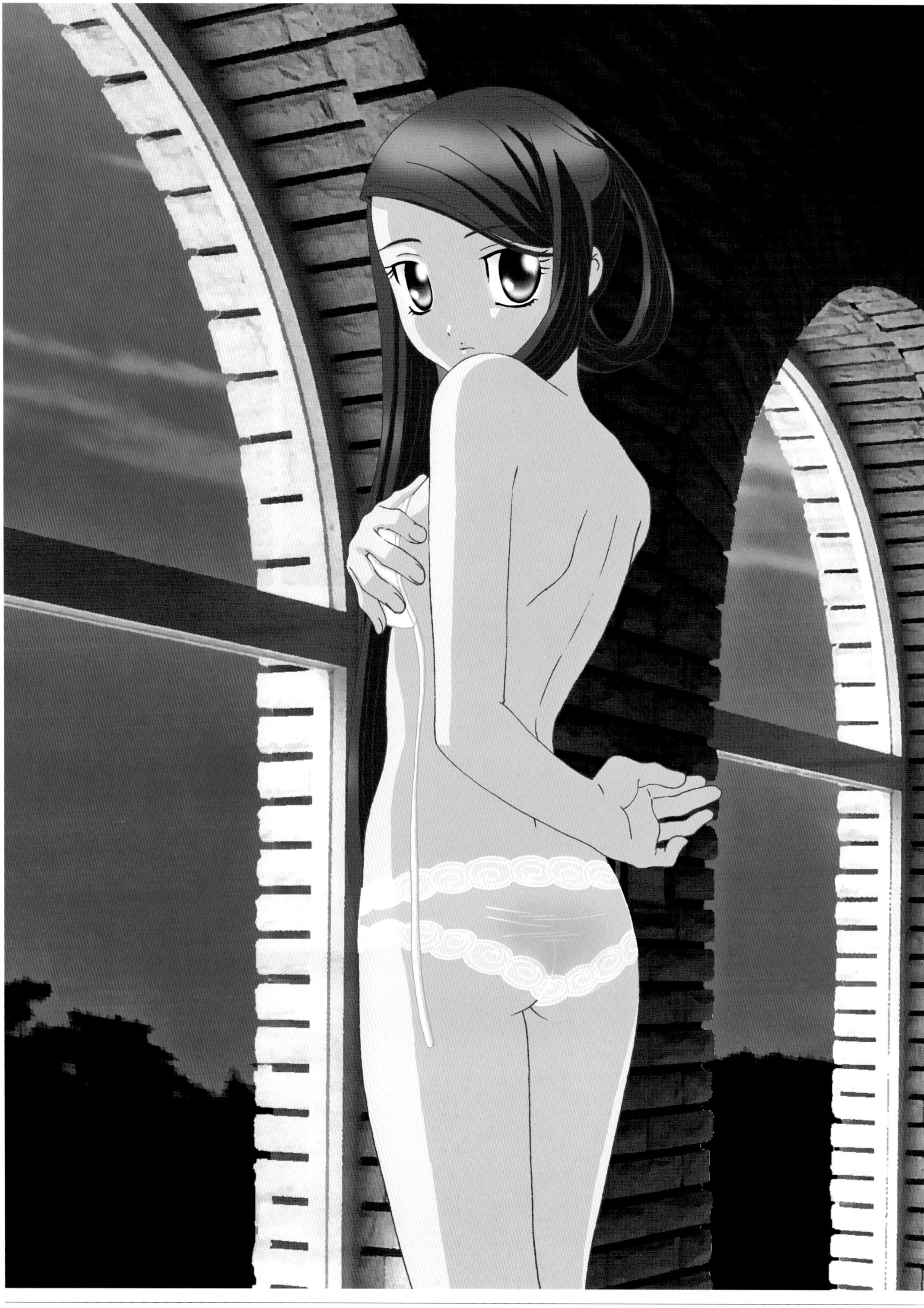

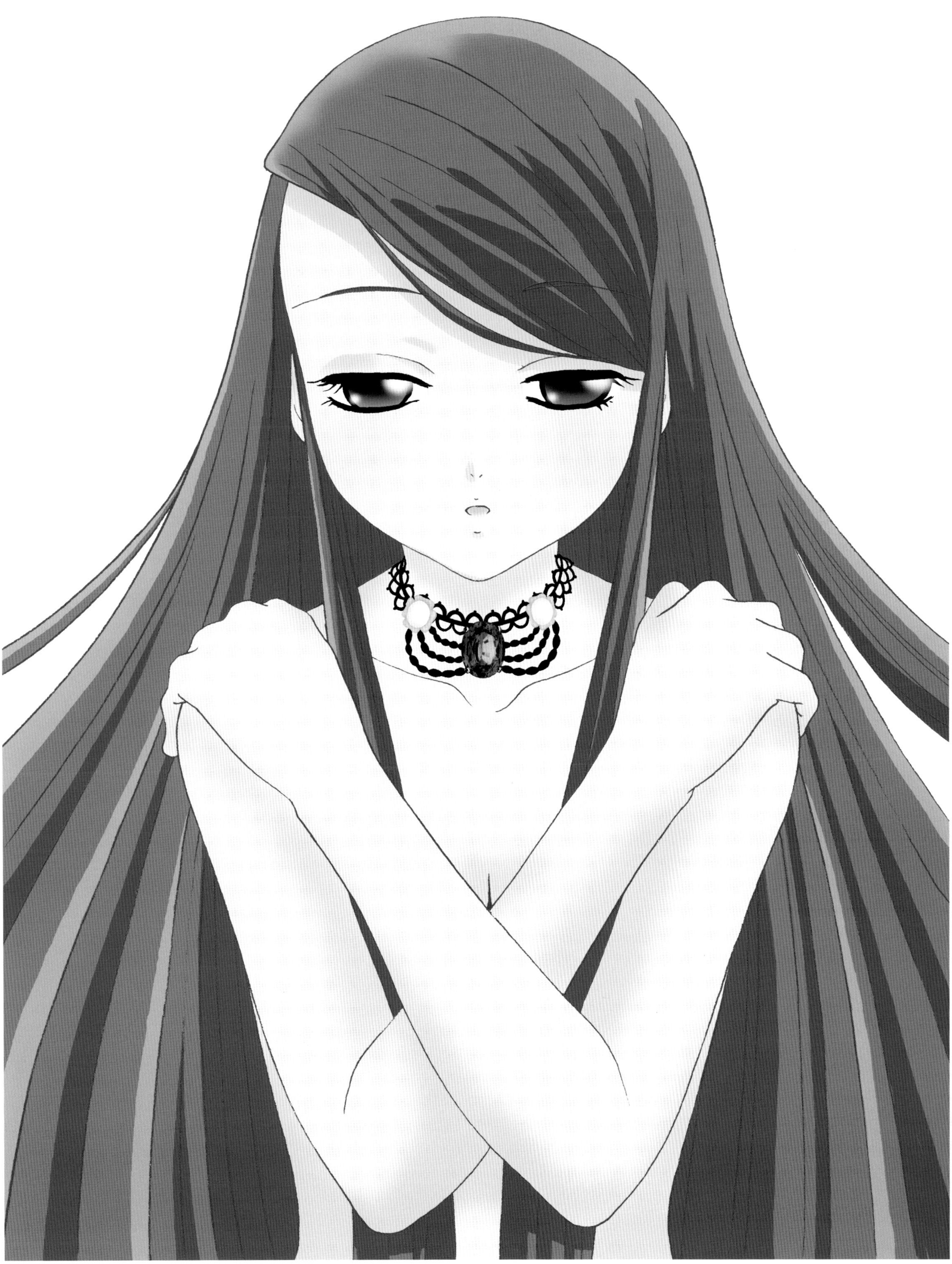

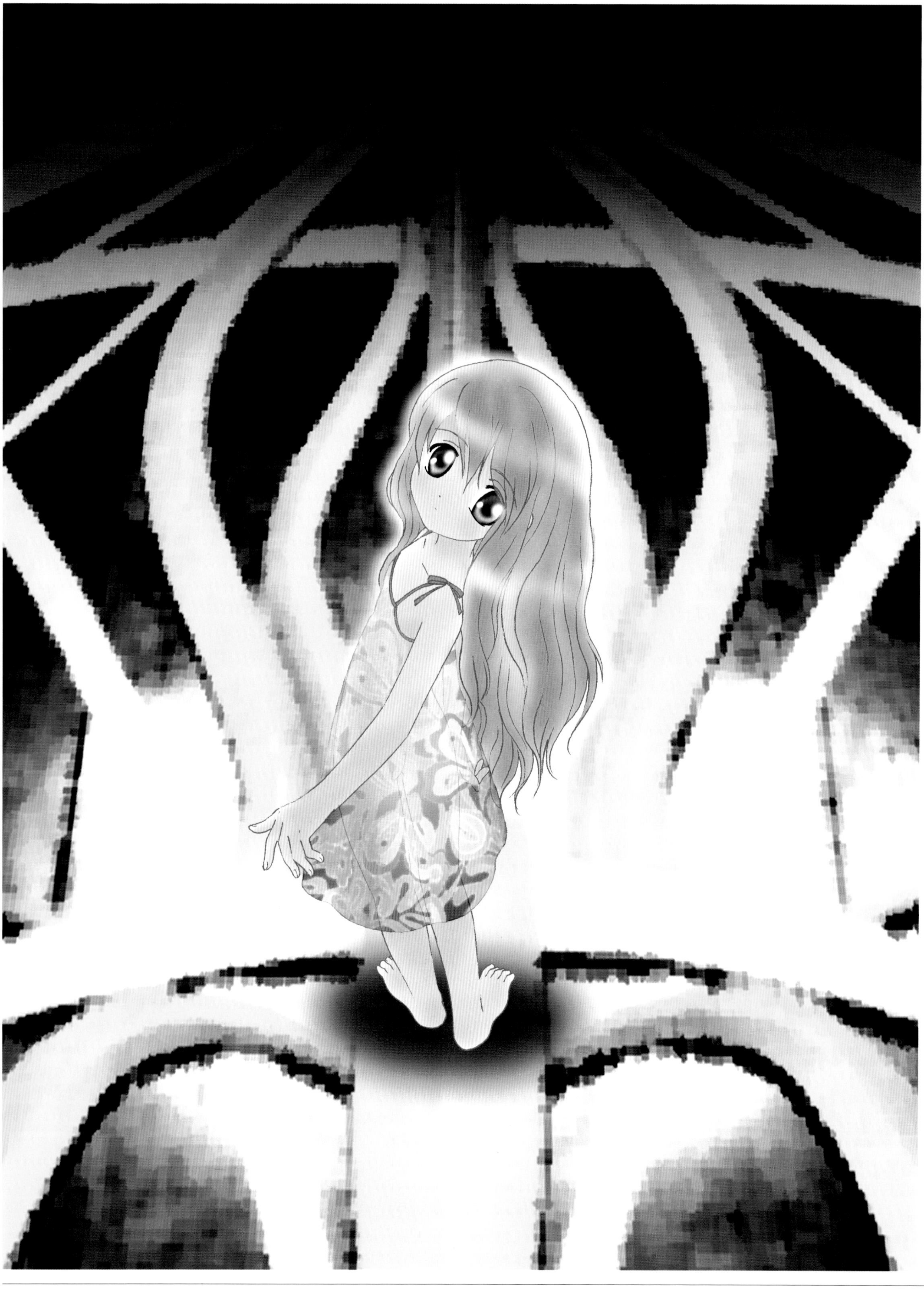

Miyu Takeshita

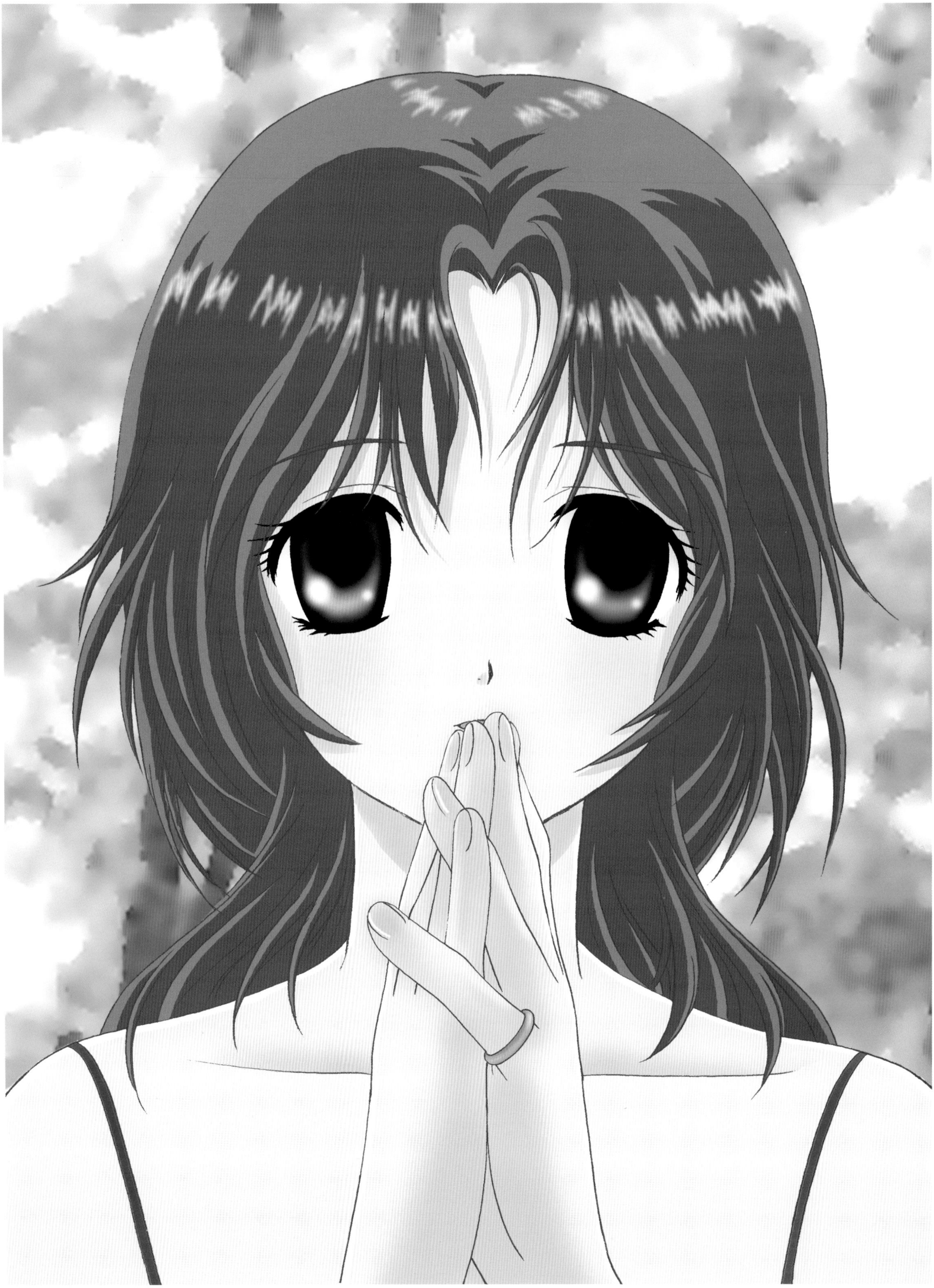

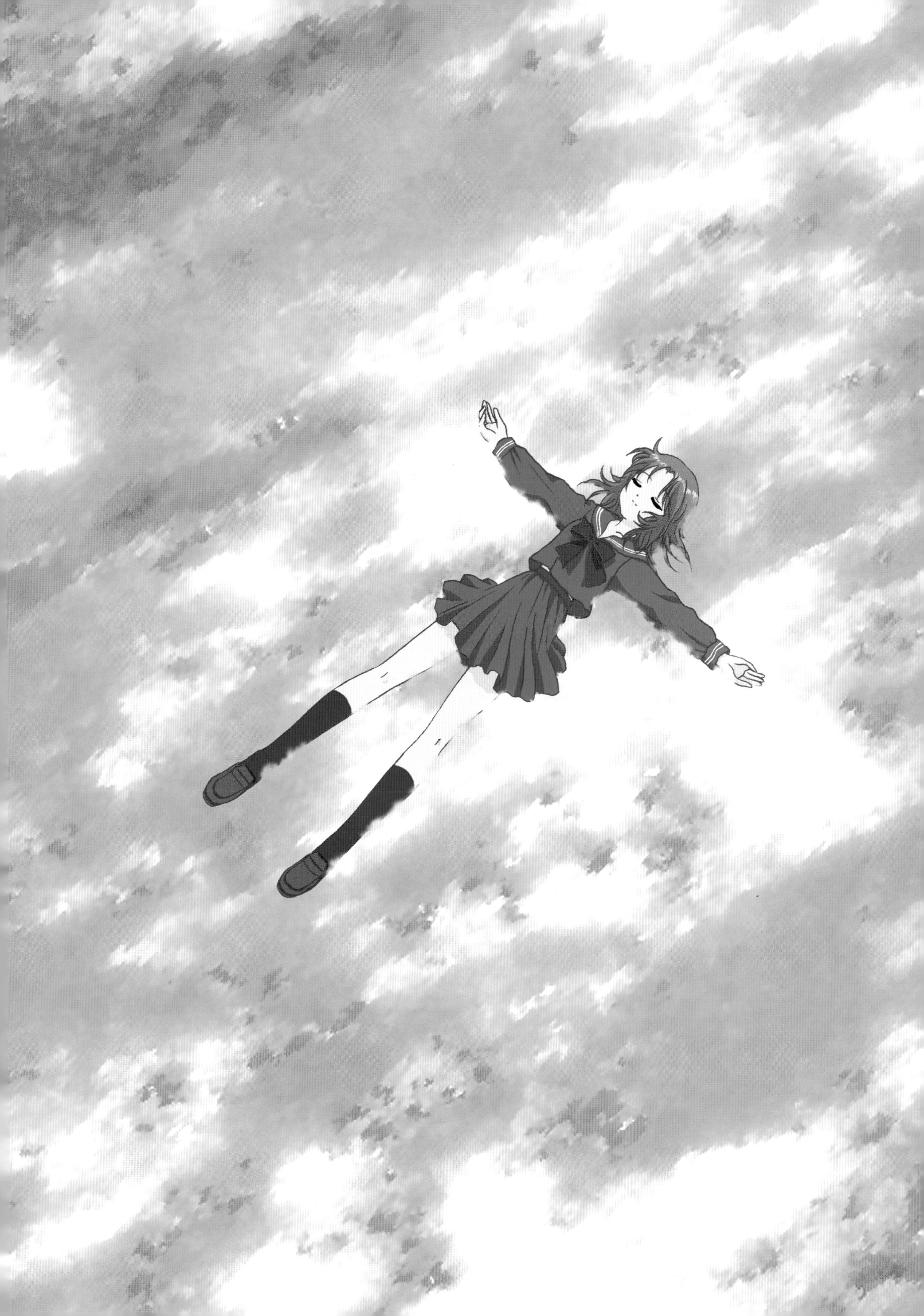

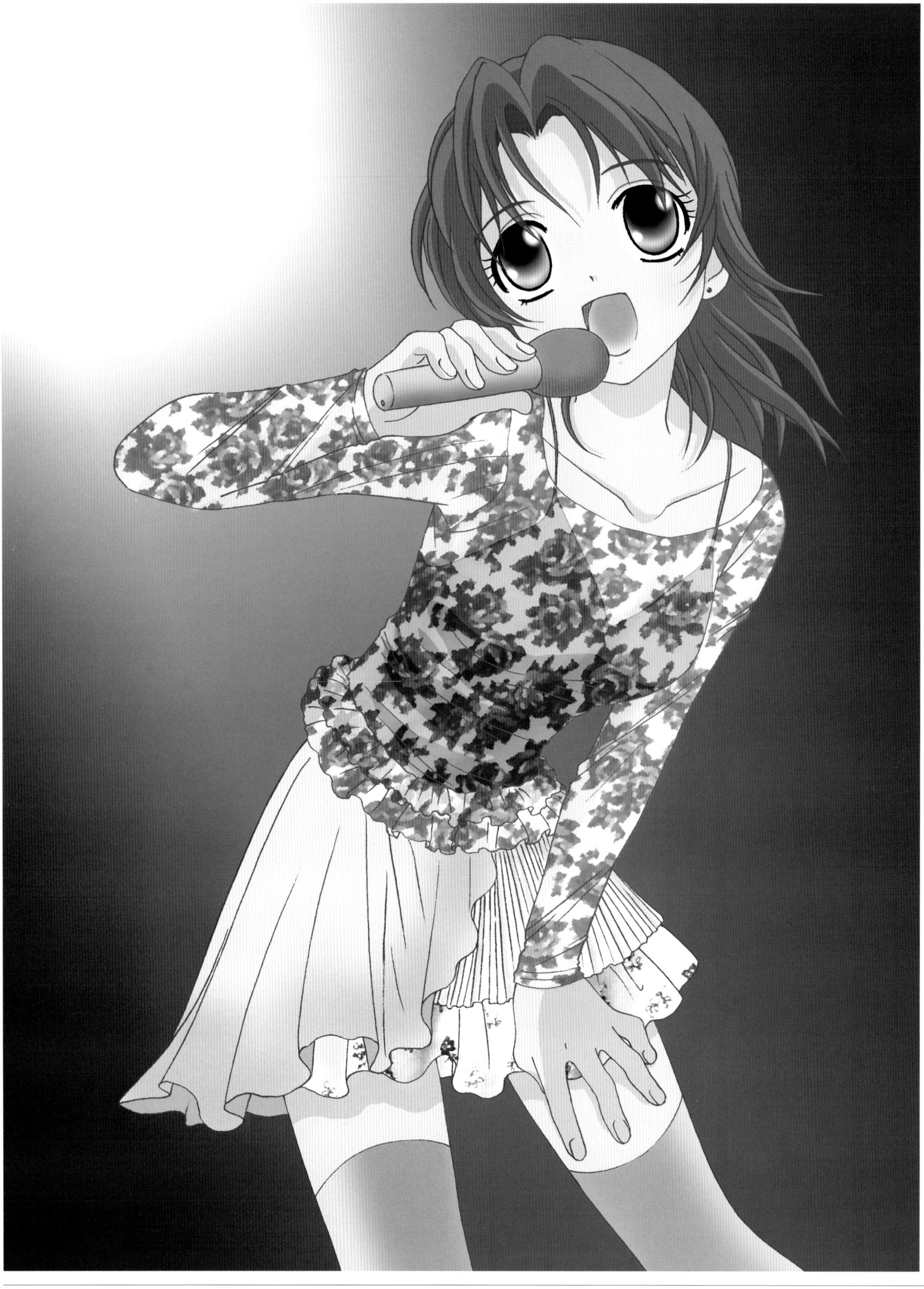

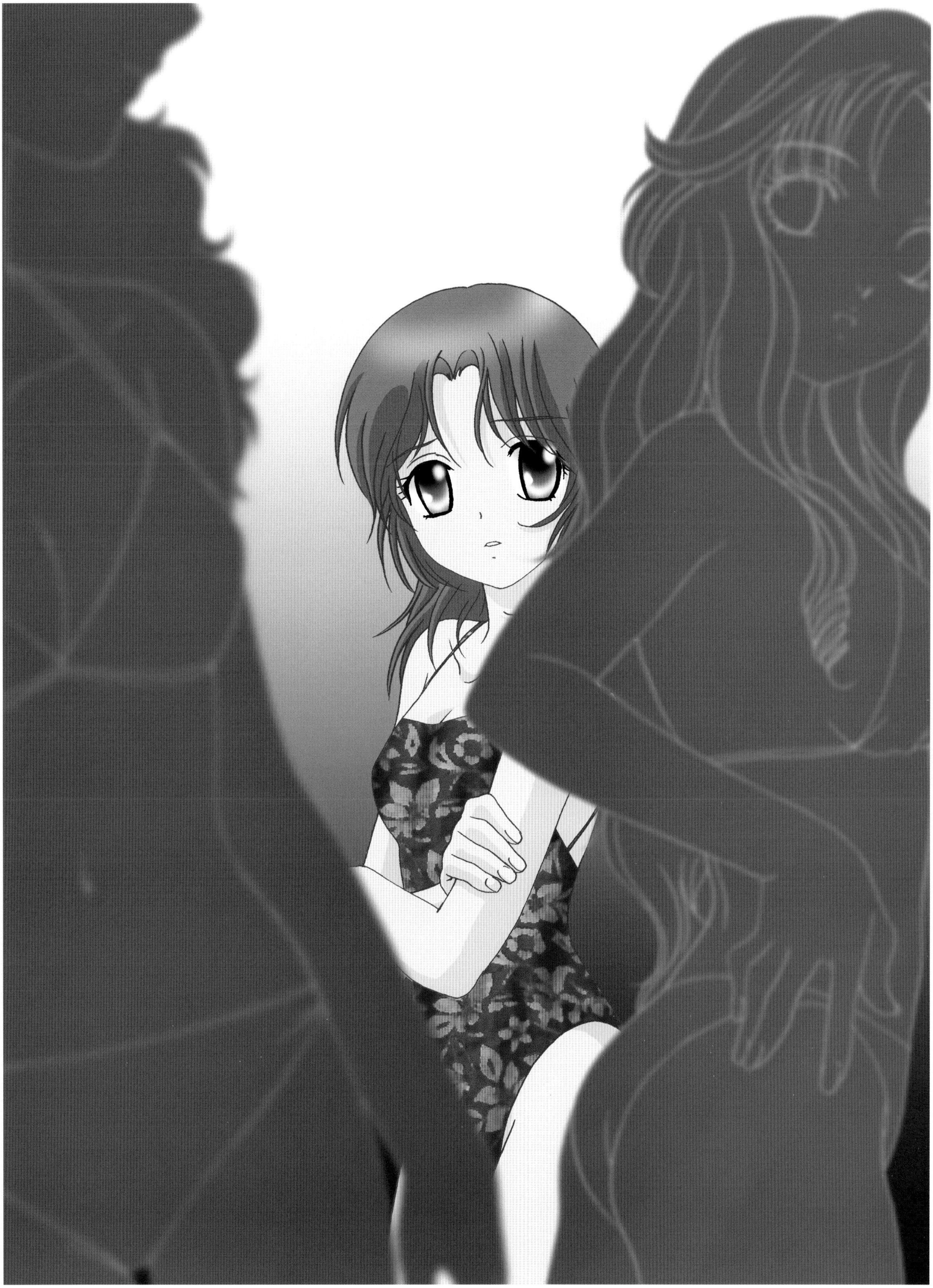

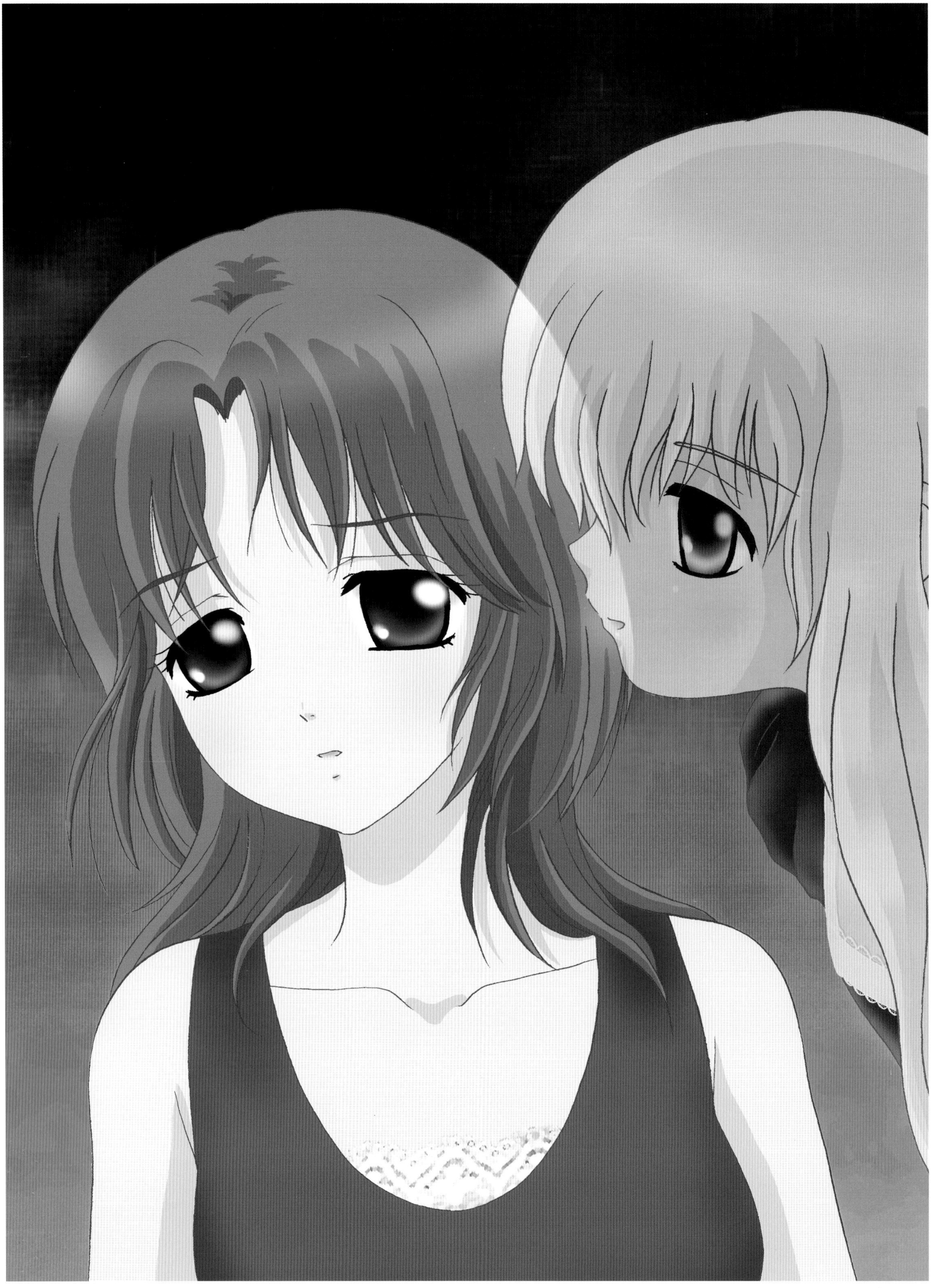

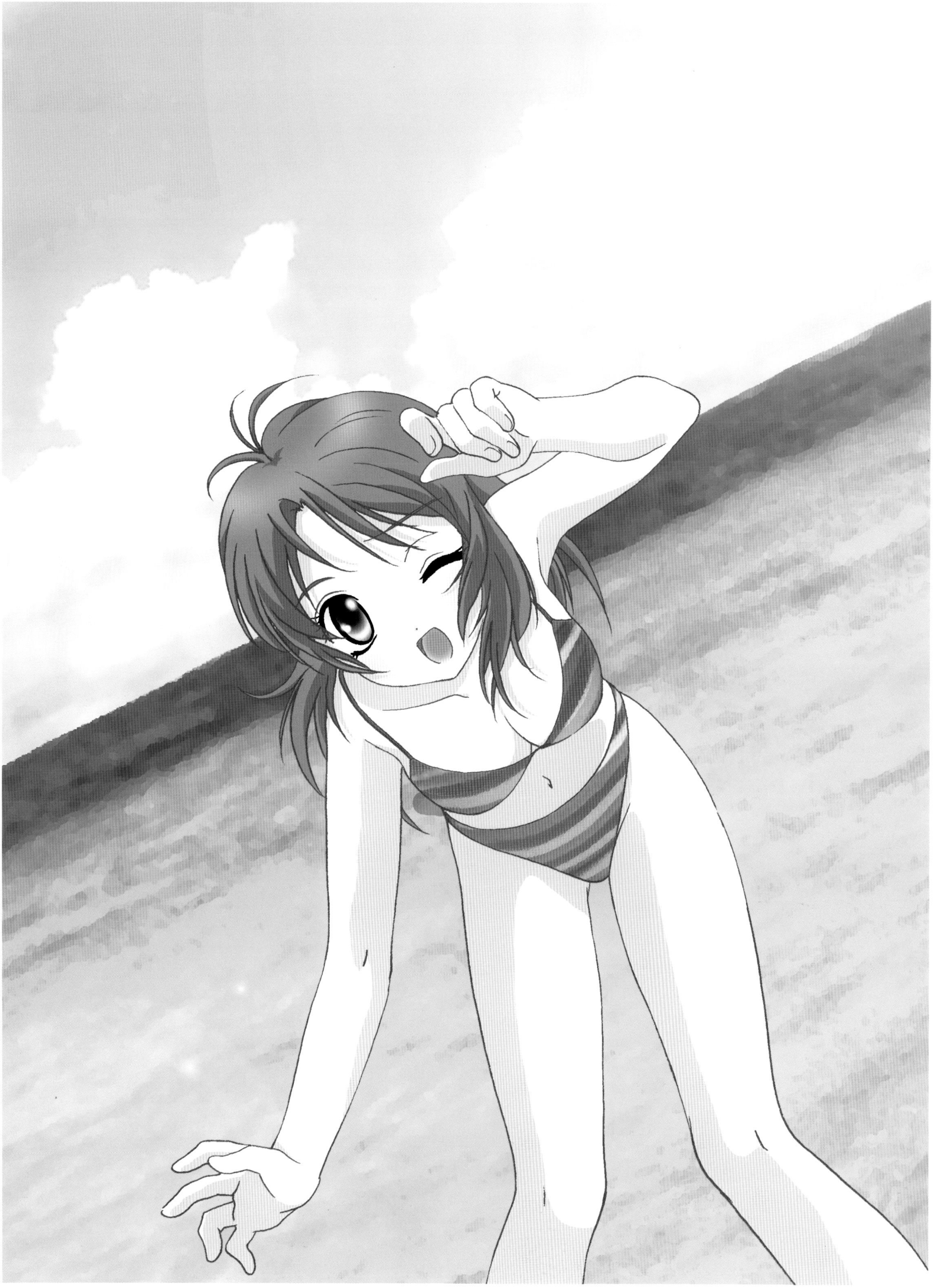

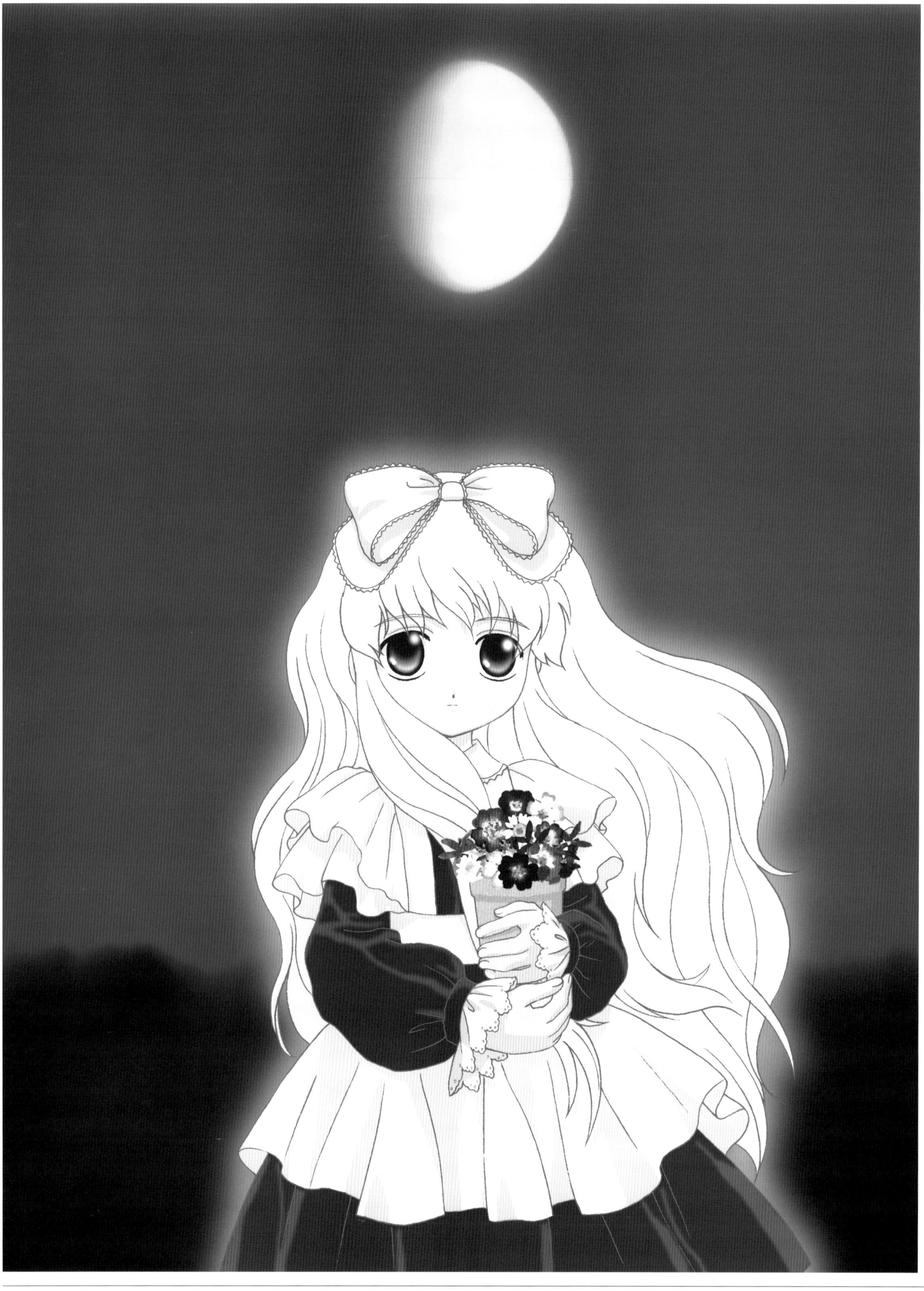

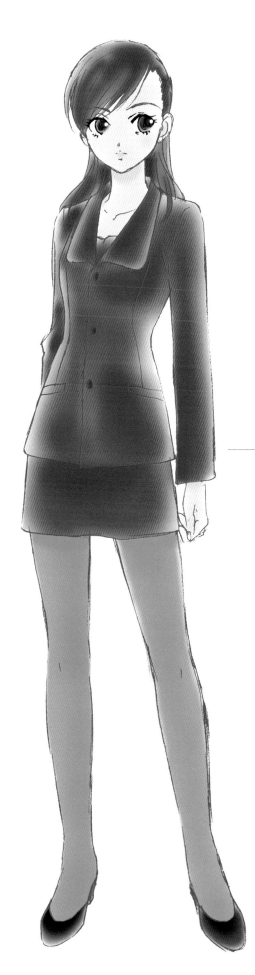

Natsuki Kubo

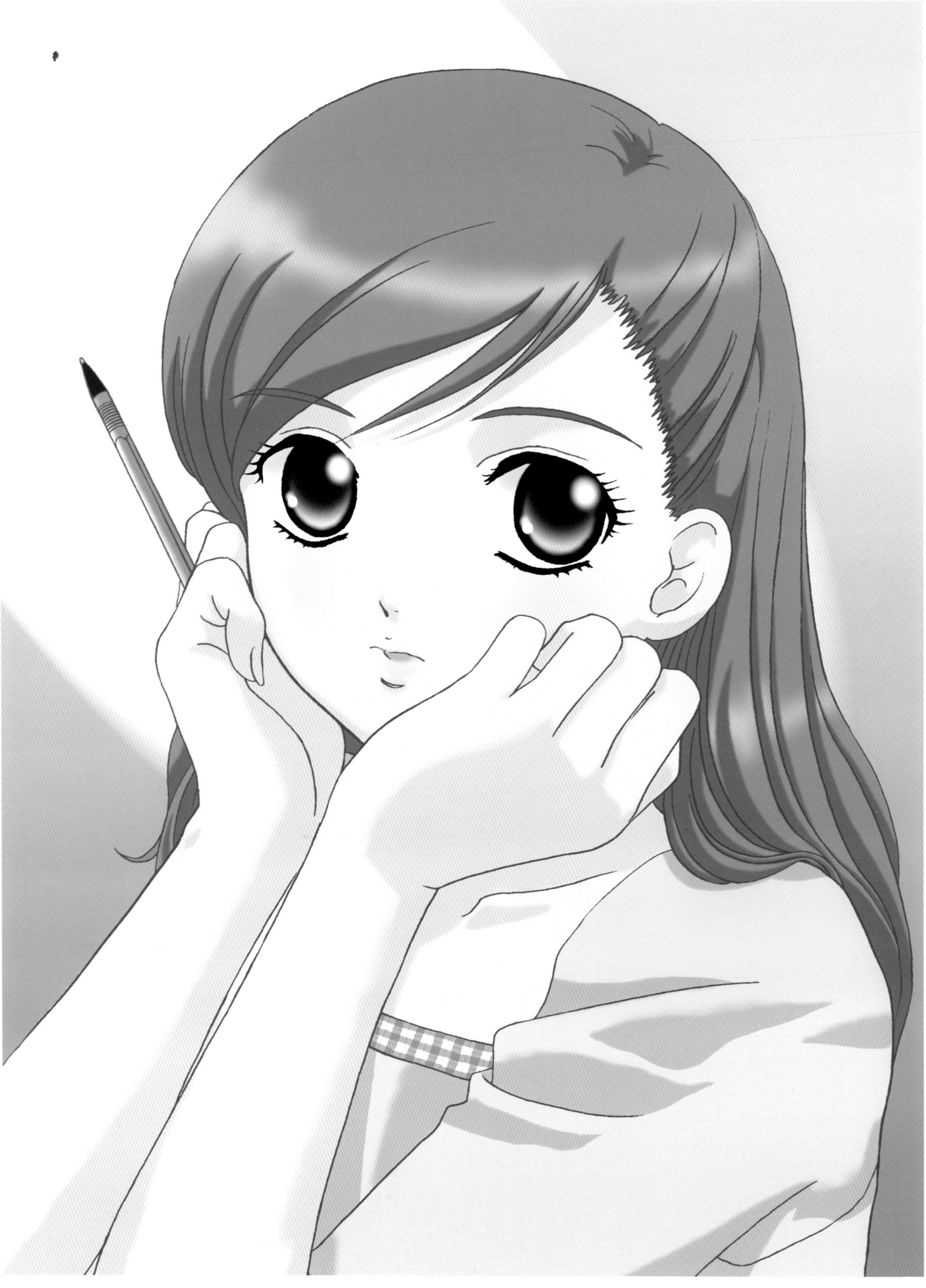

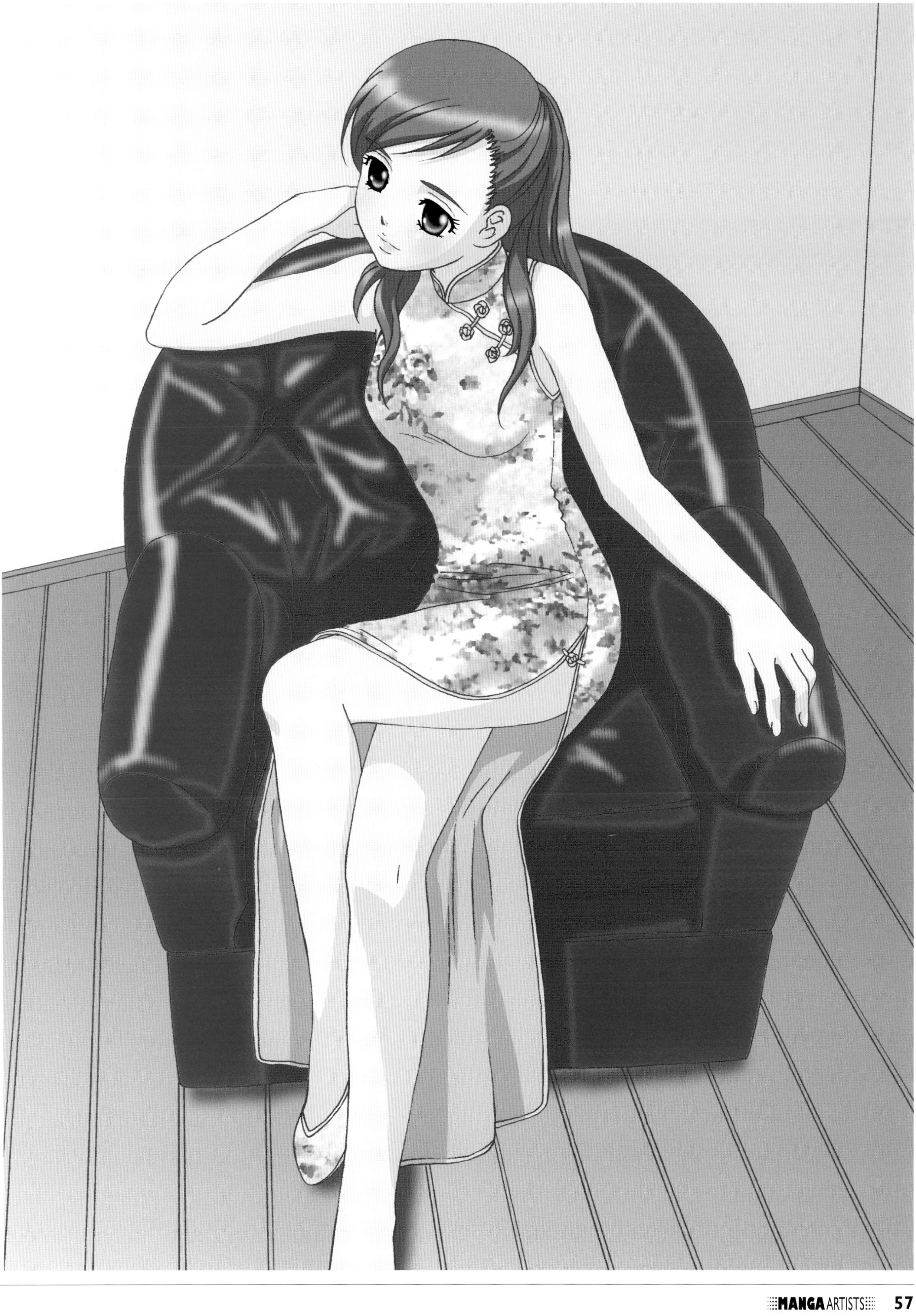

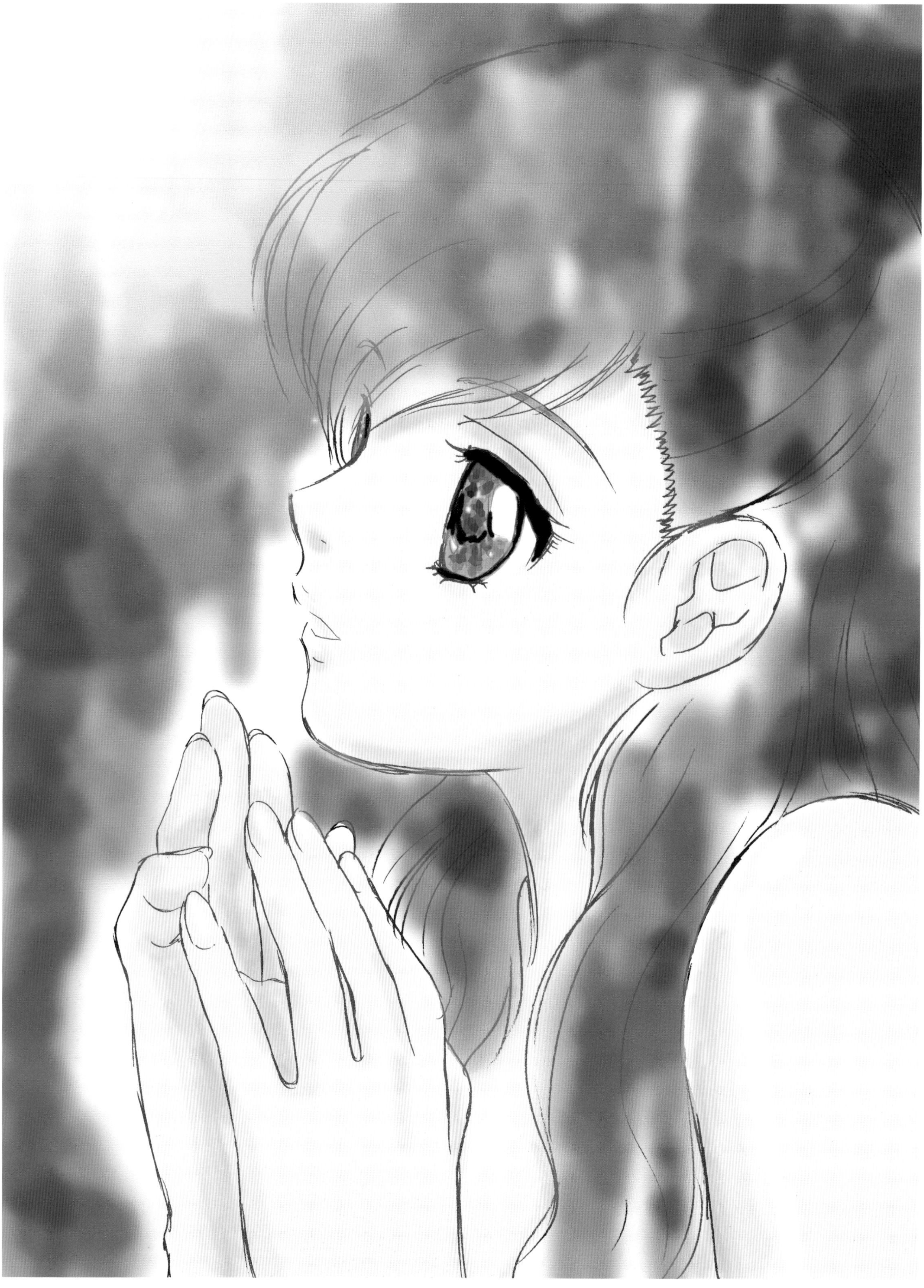

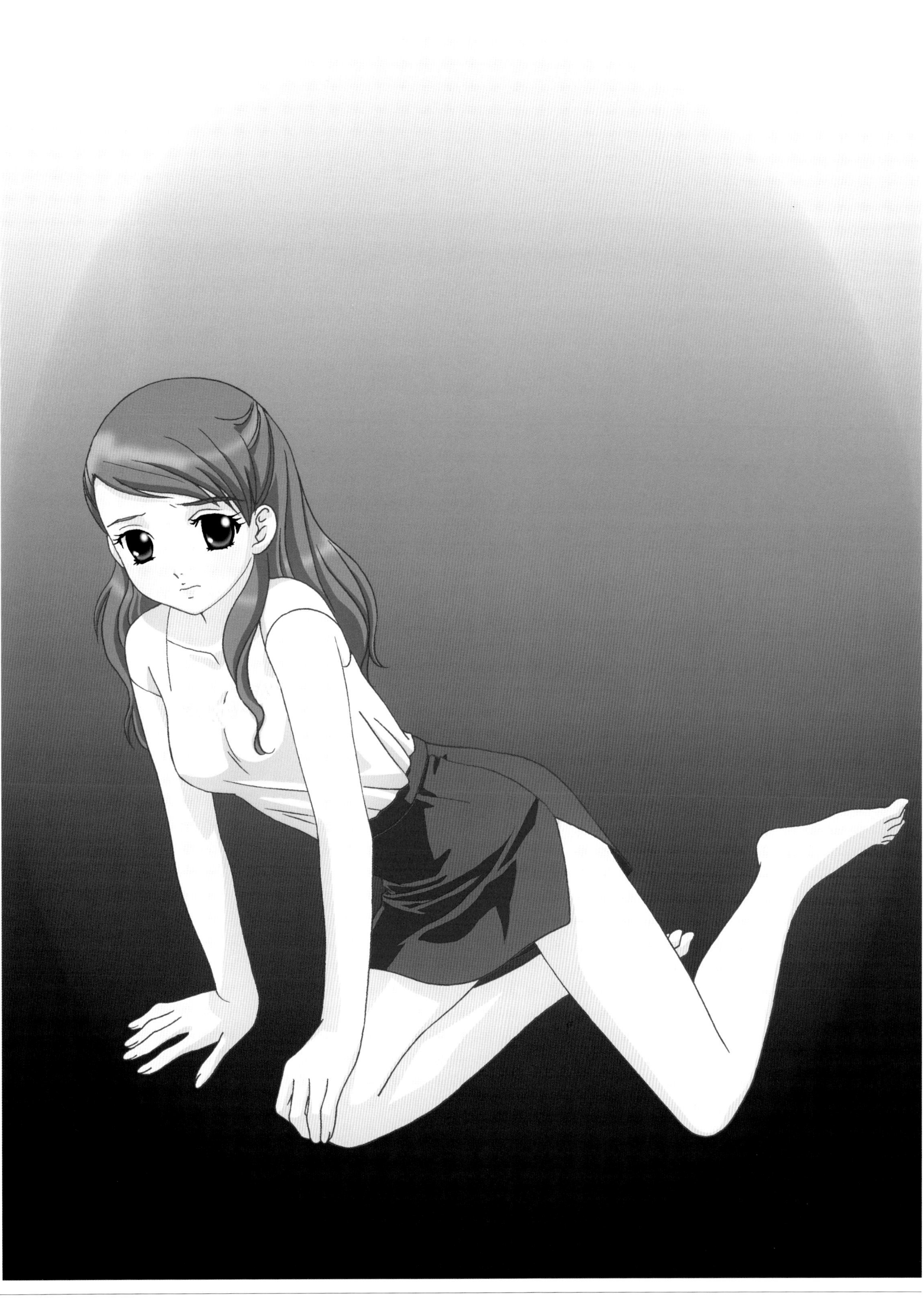

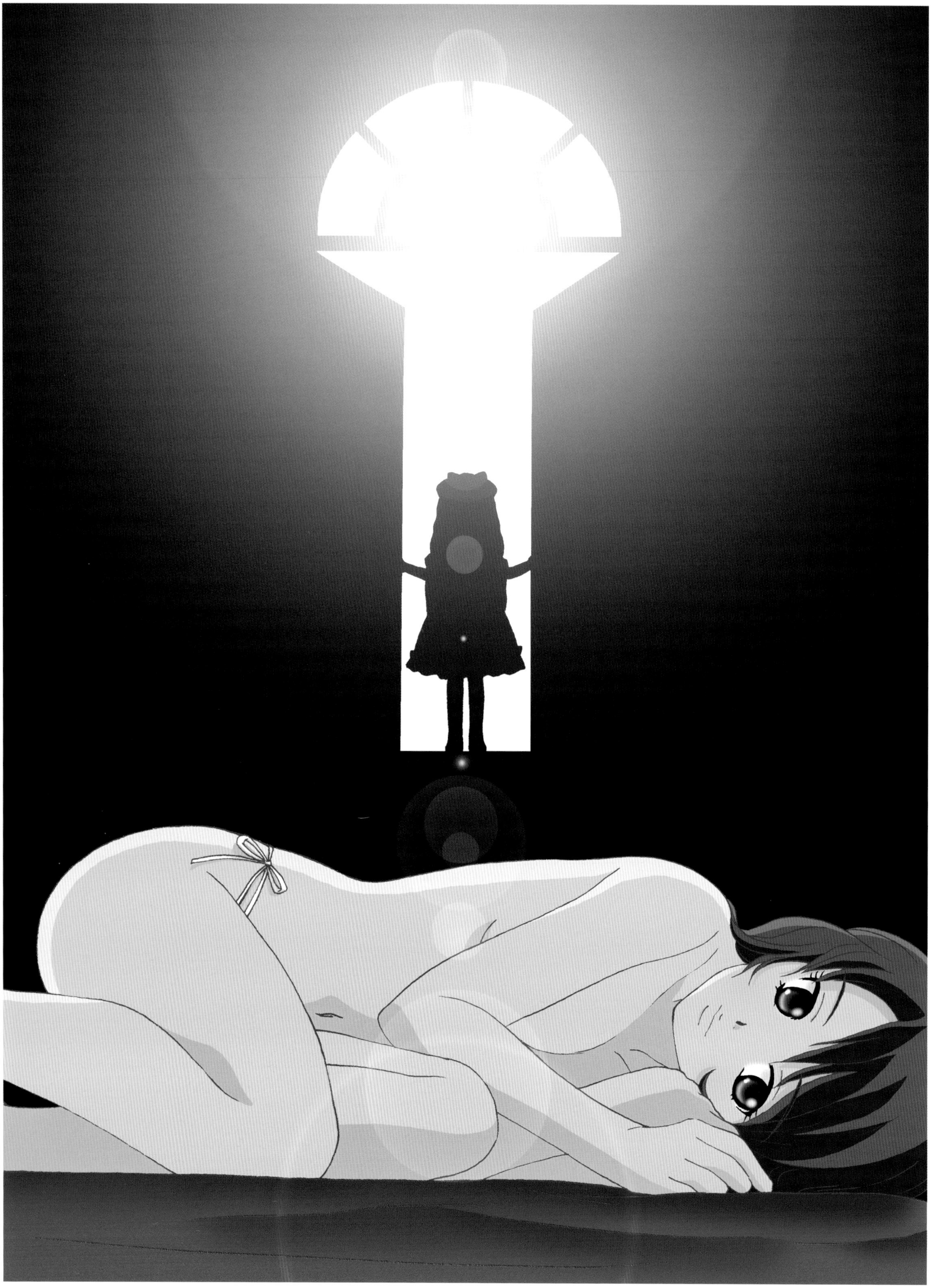

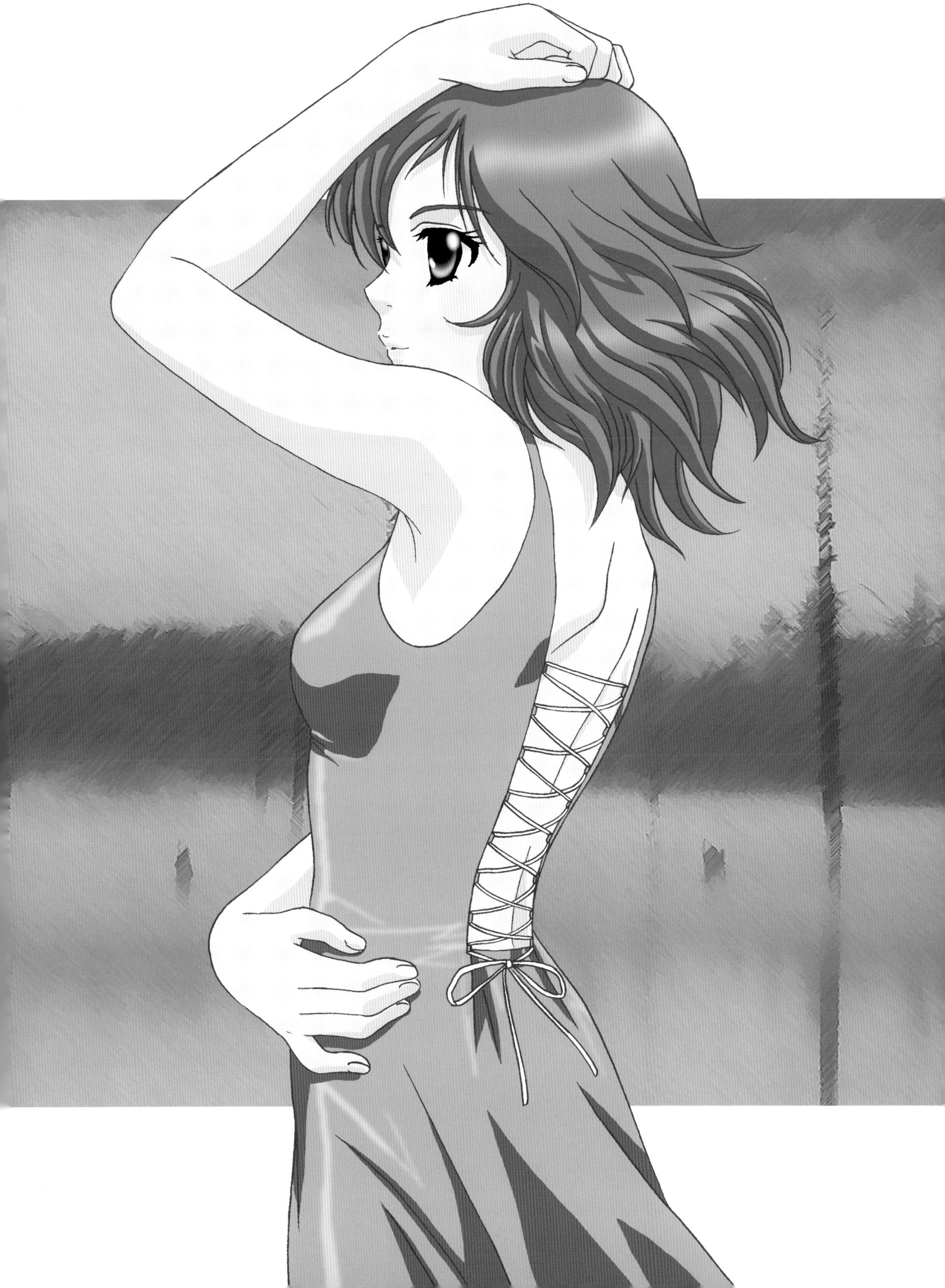

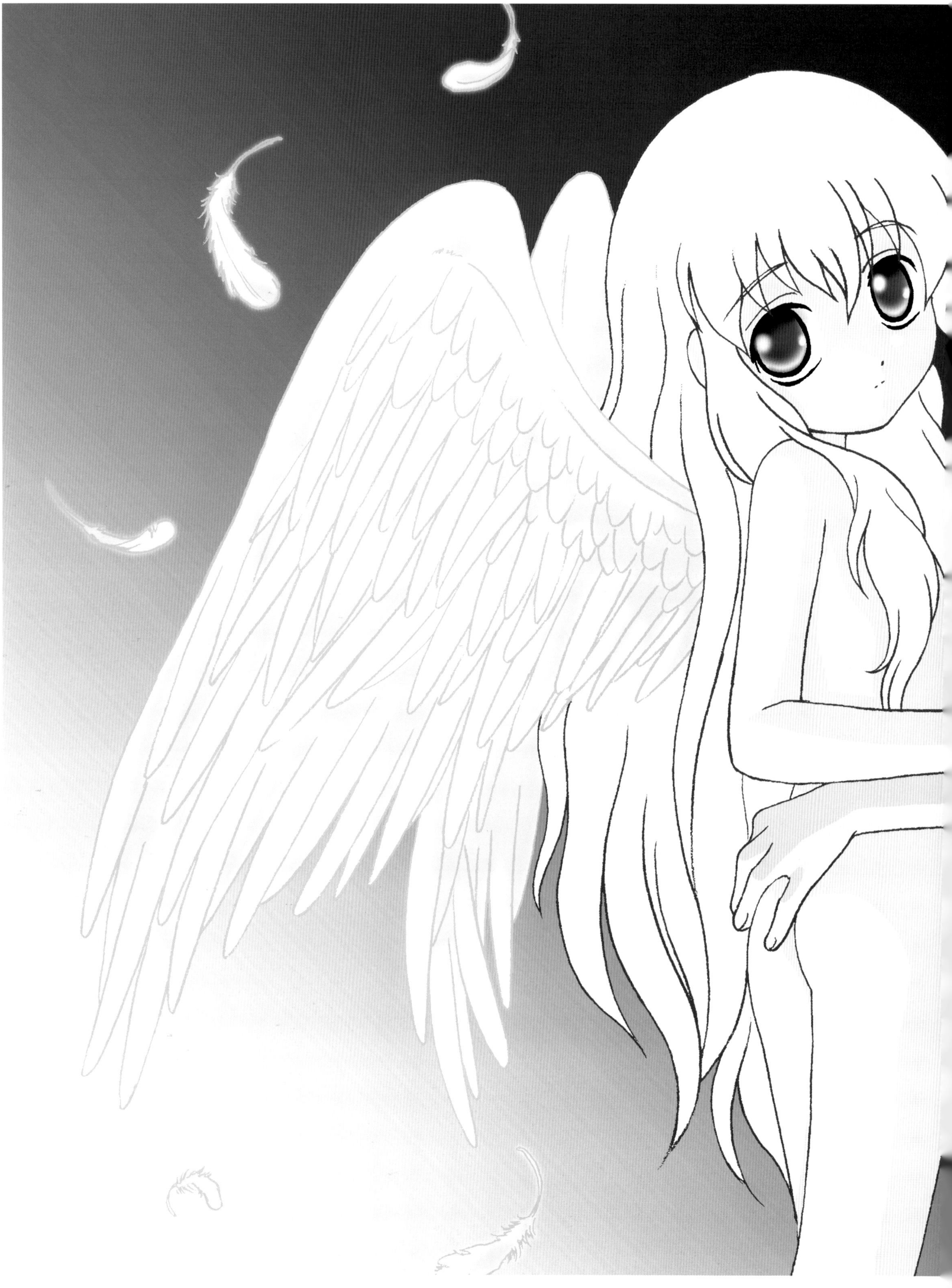

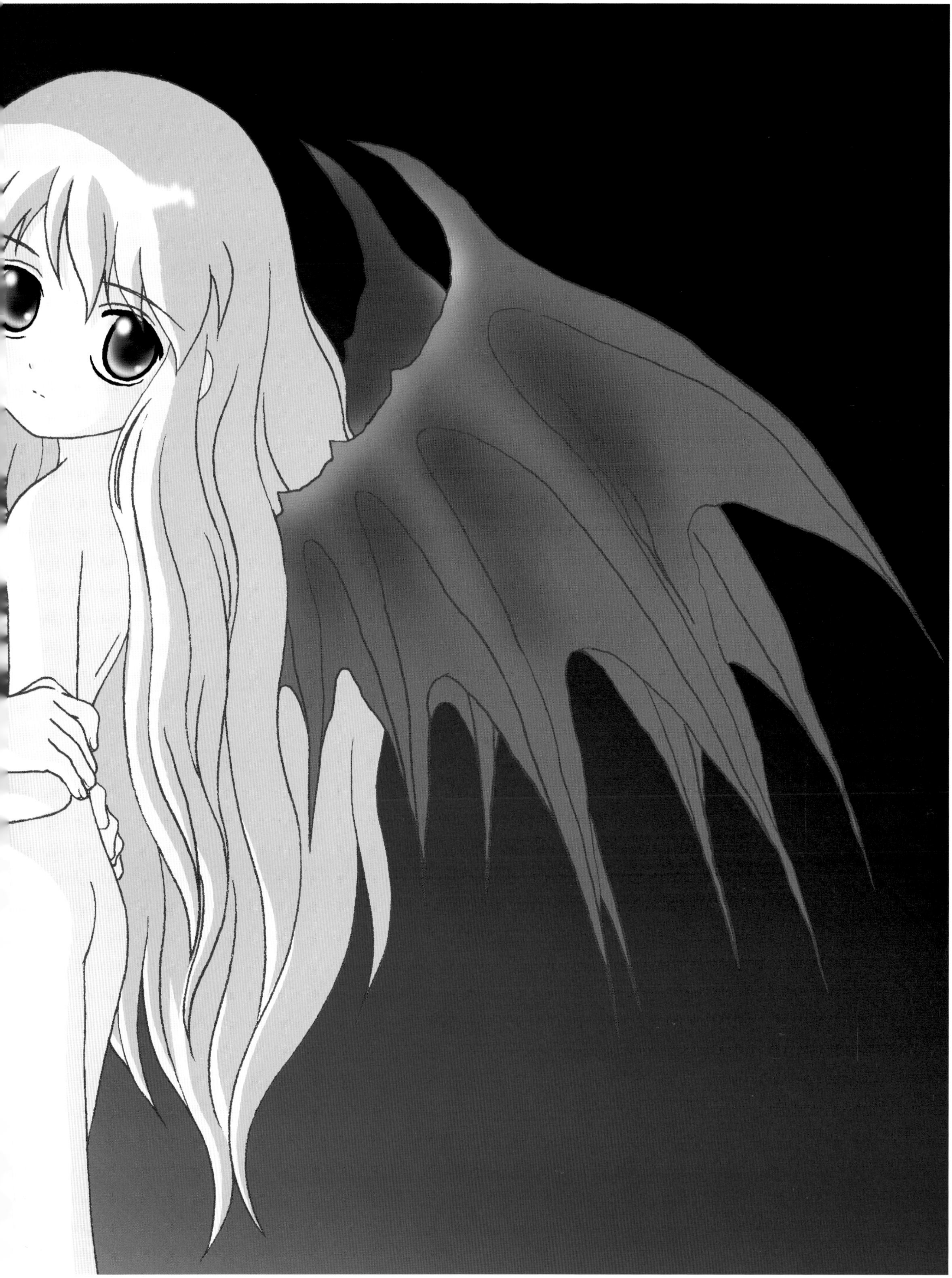

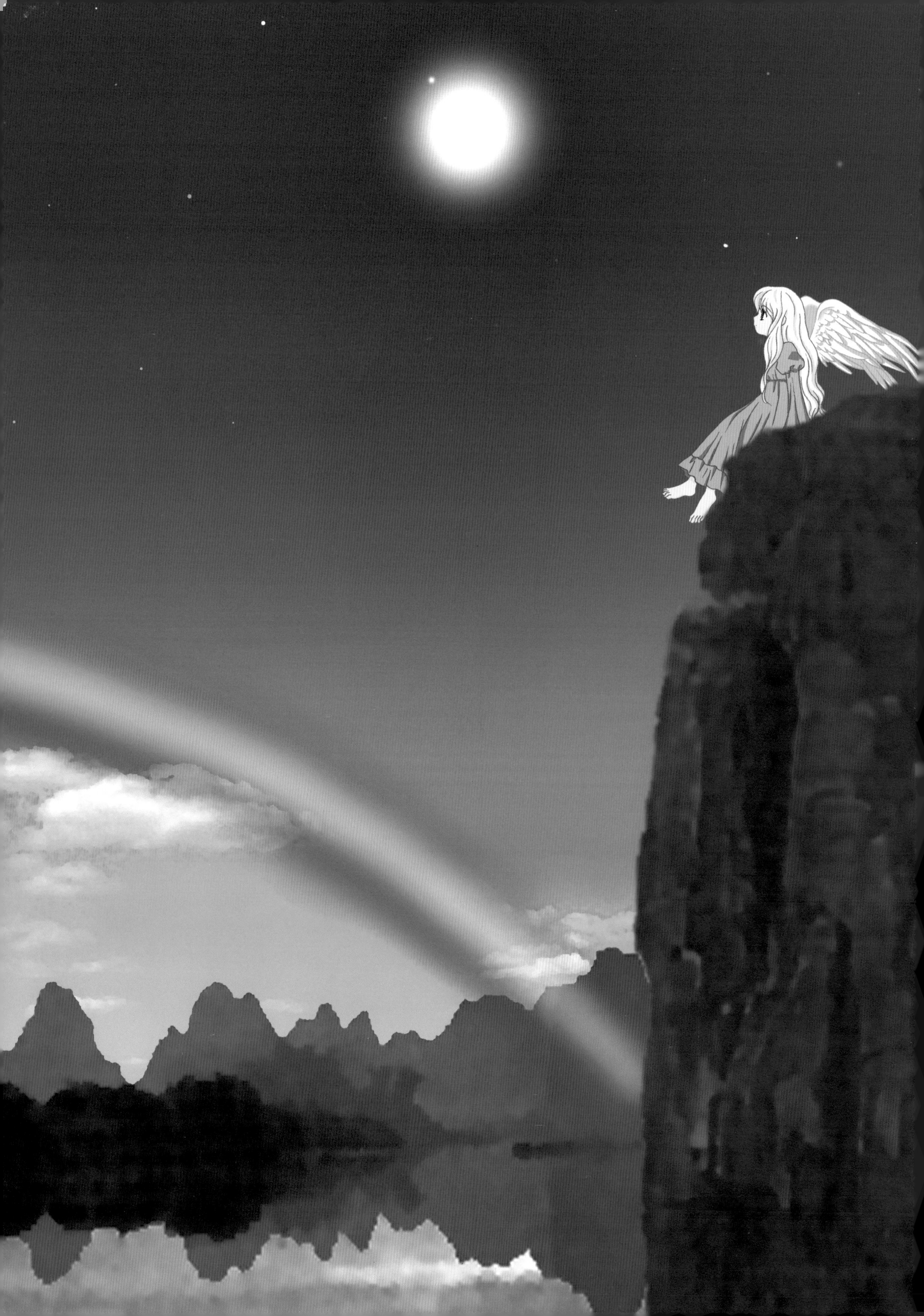

The Artist's **Sketchbook**

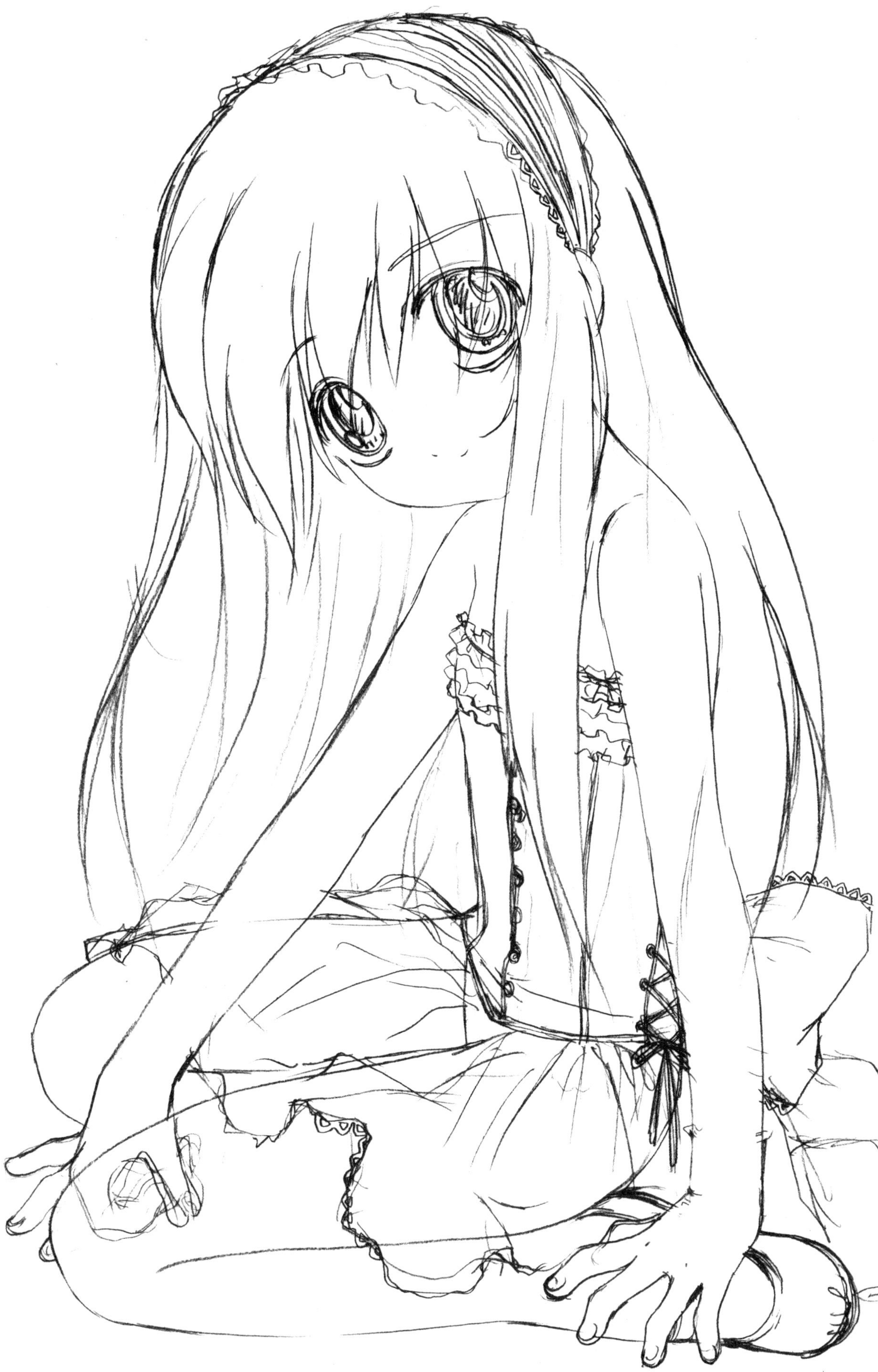

Meet a Real Kazuko Tadano Character

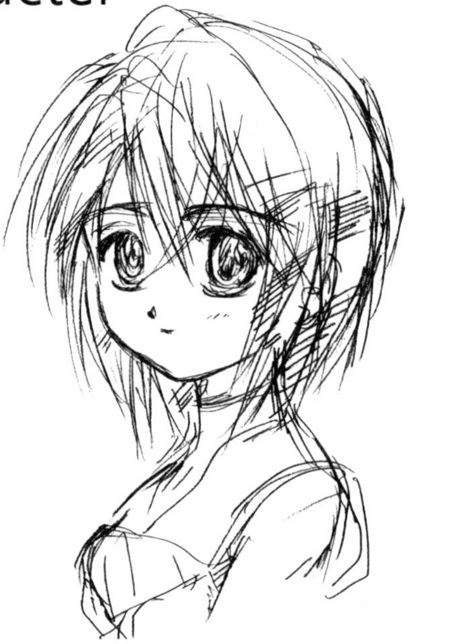

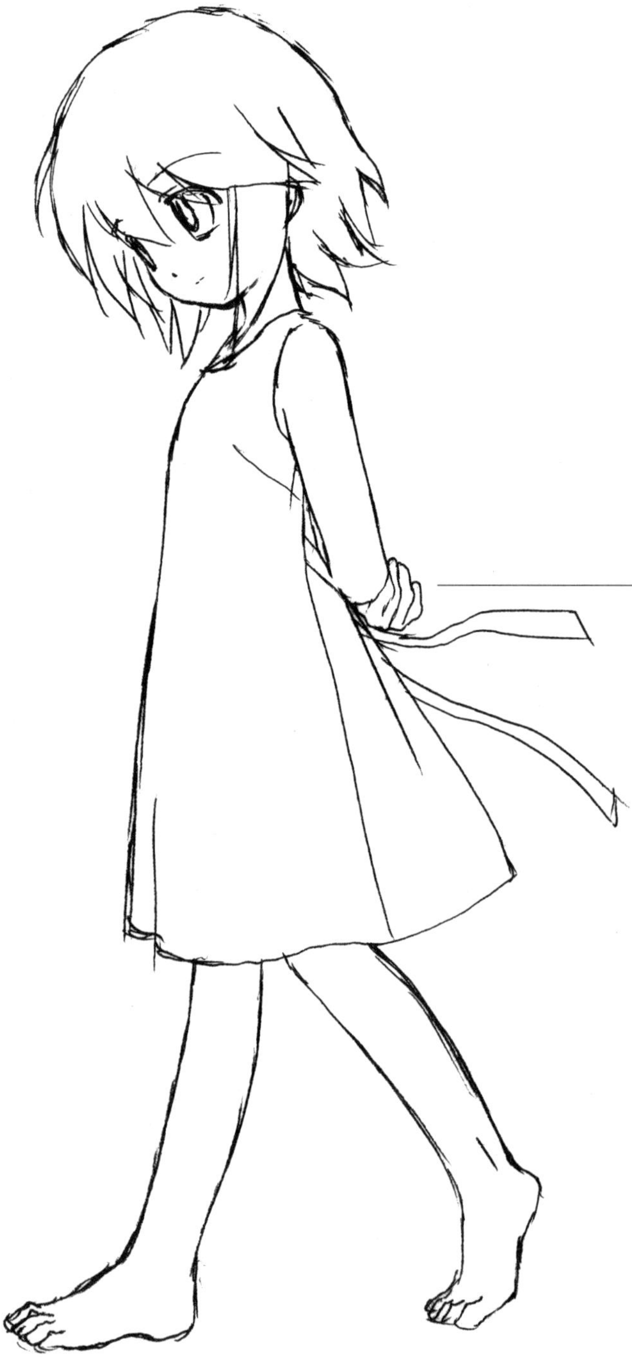

Karen Sugisaki (age 10)

Karen is a young girl who lost both parents when she was just a toddler and was raised in an orphanage. Several years later, she is adopted by a couple who operates a bakery. Yet, the normal life she so desires is still far out of her reach, and she becomes the victim of unfortunate circumstances.

—My goal was to portray a character like Oshin ["*Oshin*" *was a TV drama series aired around 1983 about a poor, little girl who someday becomes the owner of a large supermarket chain*] (I guess this is old now *laugh*), who would encounter tiny crumbs of happiness while doing her best to endure bullying and disdain from others. As a side note, I had originally designed her to be an older character.

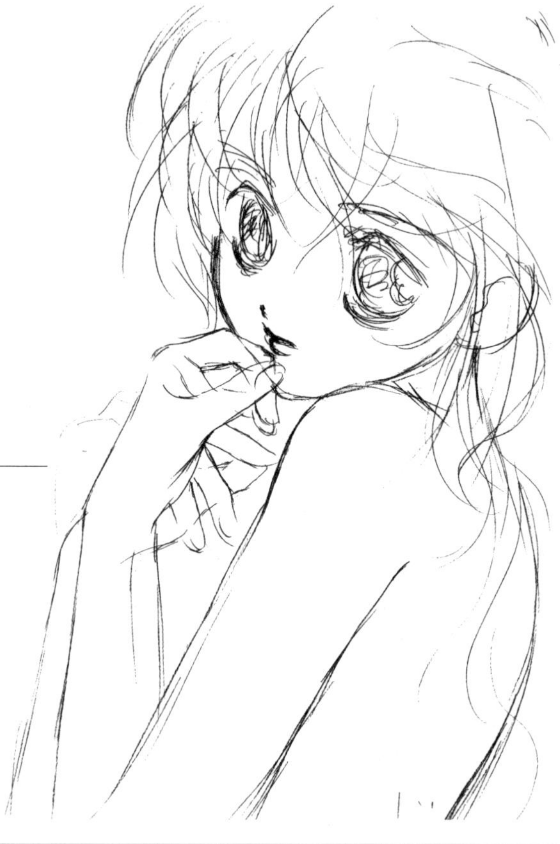

Ellémeme

(age 10; Ellémeme takes on both a black and a white incarnation)

Ellémeme is a mysterious little girl who lives inside Karen Sugisaki [see above]. Ellémeme has two aspects and depending on the beholder, Ellémeme may appear as either a sweet and pure angel or with black wings suggesting a servant of darkness.

—The two aspects of Ellémemes function to reveal the true nature of the character they inhabit, exposing those qualities not apparent based upon outward appearances. The Ellémemes appear to be playing a game through their knowledge of aspects of the story's lead that not even the lead herself recognizes, amusing themselves as the lead character grows or regresses.

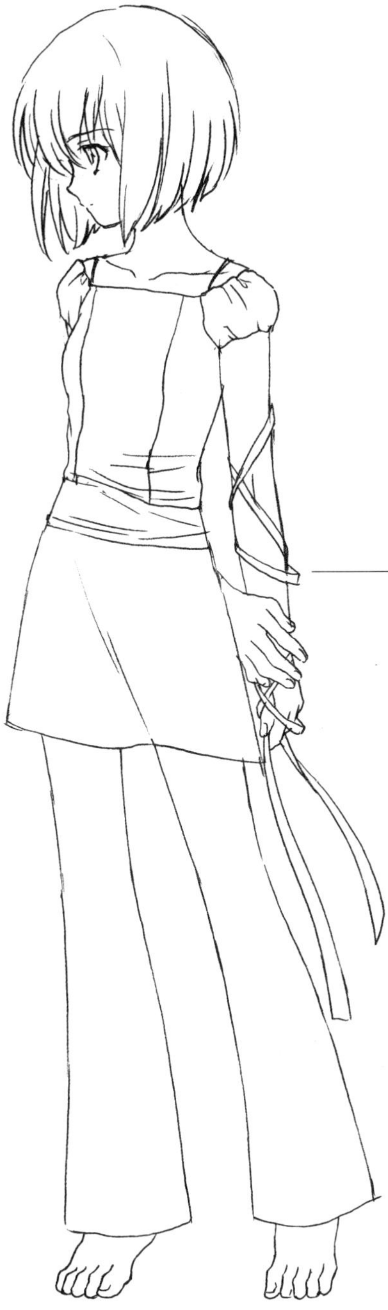

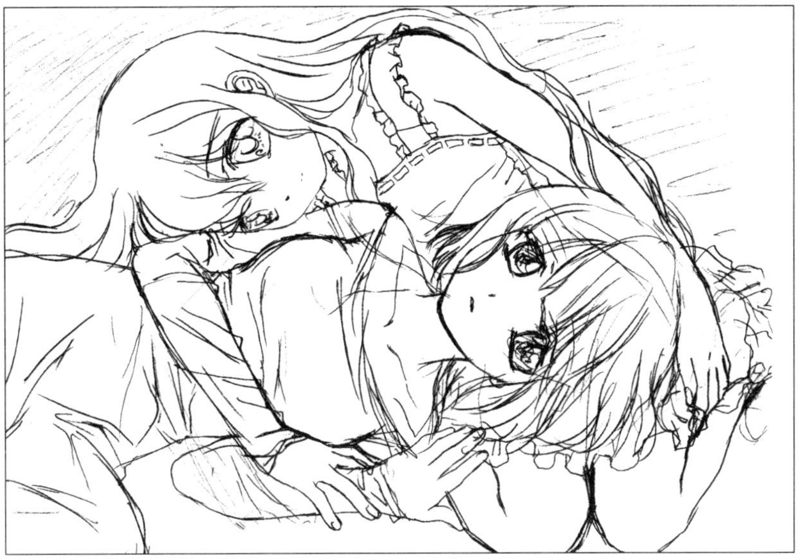

Kanako Sawada (age 19)

Kanako is a university student who came from a small town to Tokyo and is now living by herself. She was trying to maintain a long-distance relationship, but living in the big city has caused her sense of values to take a 180-degree turn. She experiences a brief moment of happiness, but feels a great loss when the magic of the moment evaporates. The frailty of interpersonal relationships gradually erodes her emotional state, while she experiences sleepless night after sleepless night.

—My intention was to express with this character the difficulty in overcoming one's first taste of loneliness in living by oneself and leading a dissatisfying lifestyle.

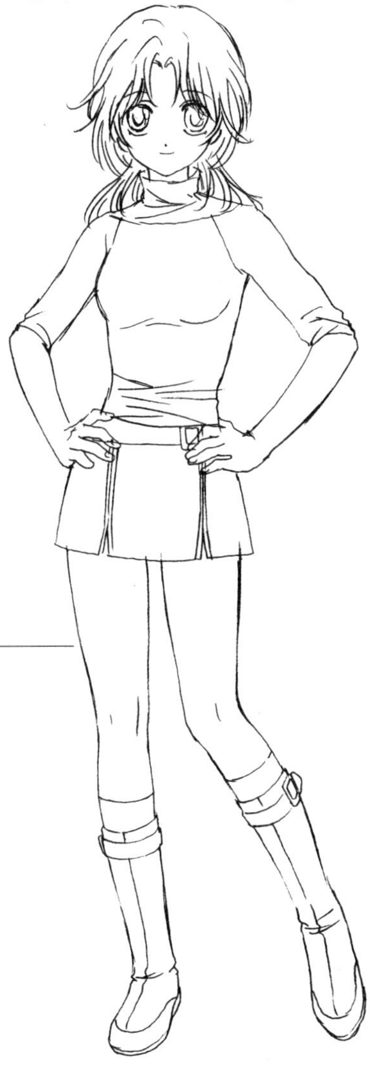

Miyu Takeshita (age 17)

Miyu is a rising talent seeking to become a star. She has gone through countless auditions, only to be turned down, Meanwhile, she has witnessed others who started later surpass her, causing Miyu to lose her self-confidence. One day, she catches several younger actresses making fun of her behind her back and has a falling out with her friends over a lie that just pops out of Miyu's mouth. Things turn around for Miyu, and she finds herself selected as a lead role.

—Here we have a character who projects superficially a bright and gay performance yet underneath her exterior we see her emotions made murky in a complicated intertwining of jealousy and desire. My intention with this character was to take an innocent young girl and have her experience the cruel lessons in life.

Key Points in Producing Illustrations the Kazuko Tadano Way

The Eyes

The crucial element to the "Tadano style" lies in the pupils and irises. I draw the characters' eyes relatively large. While on the one hand, this allows me to portray their emotional state more readily, large irises are just plain cute (laugh).

I modify the impression the character projects by increasing or reducing the volume of eyelashes. In the cases of Karen or Ellémeme, I wanted to play down the sense of a coquettish feminine character, so I omitted the eyelashes altogether.

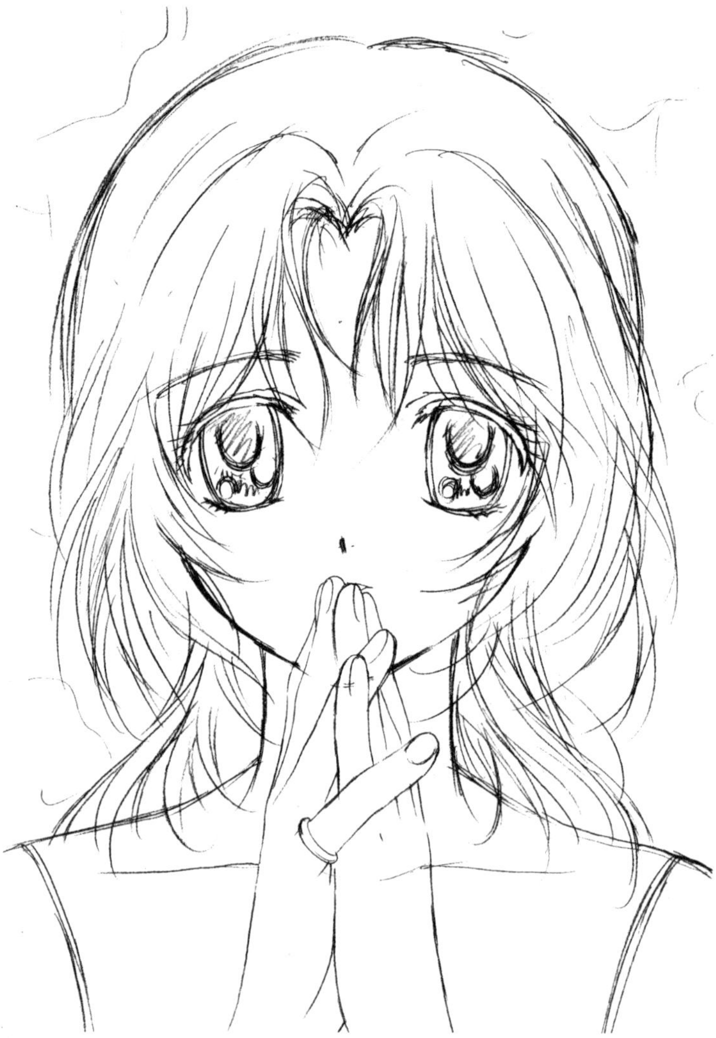

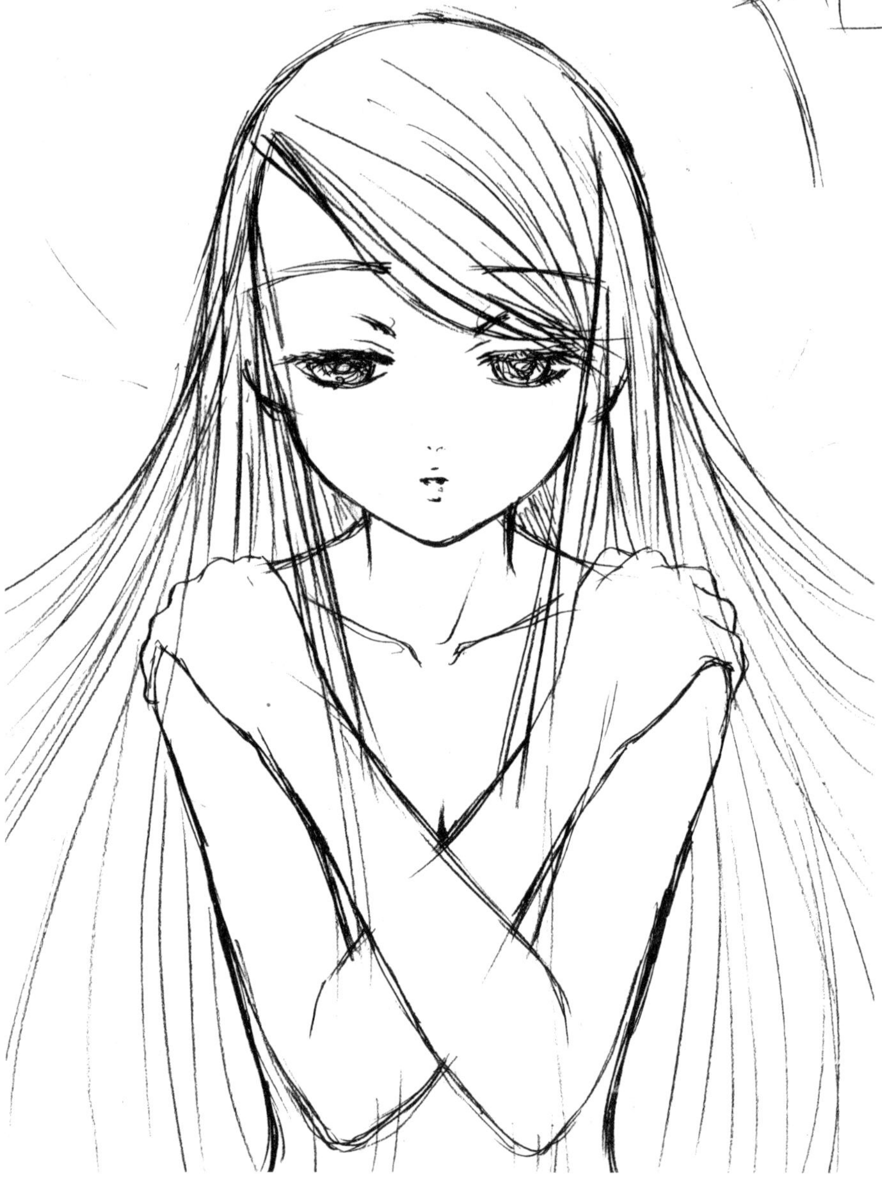

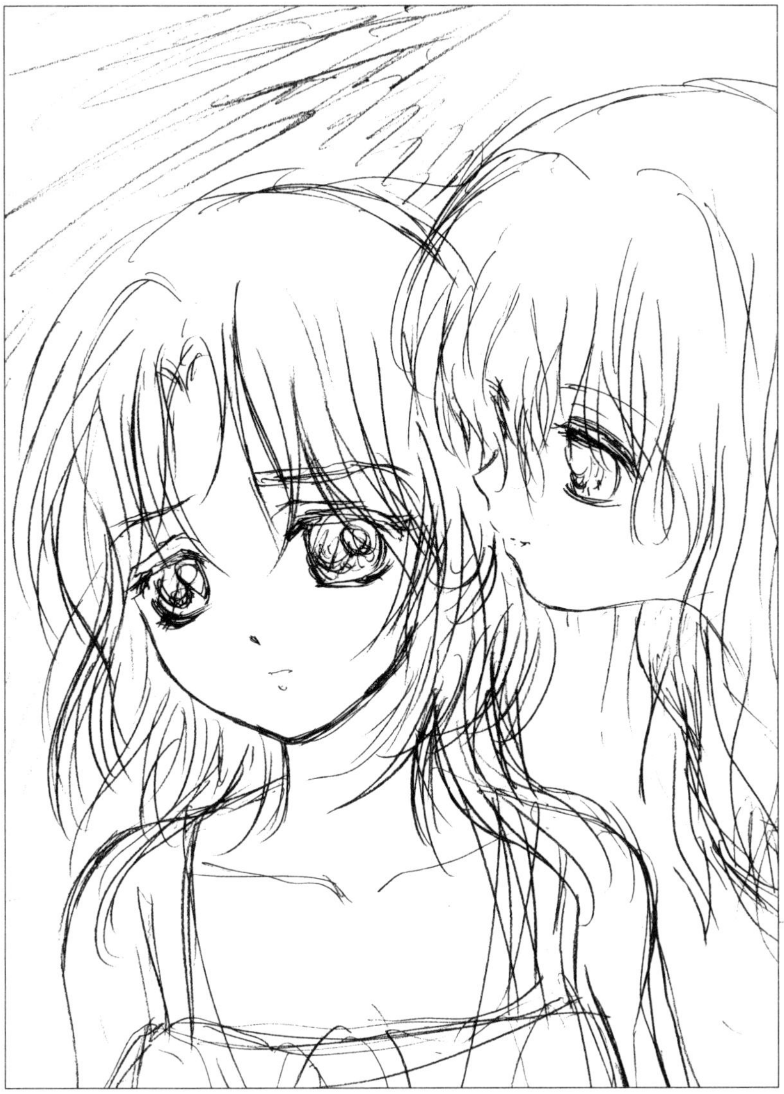

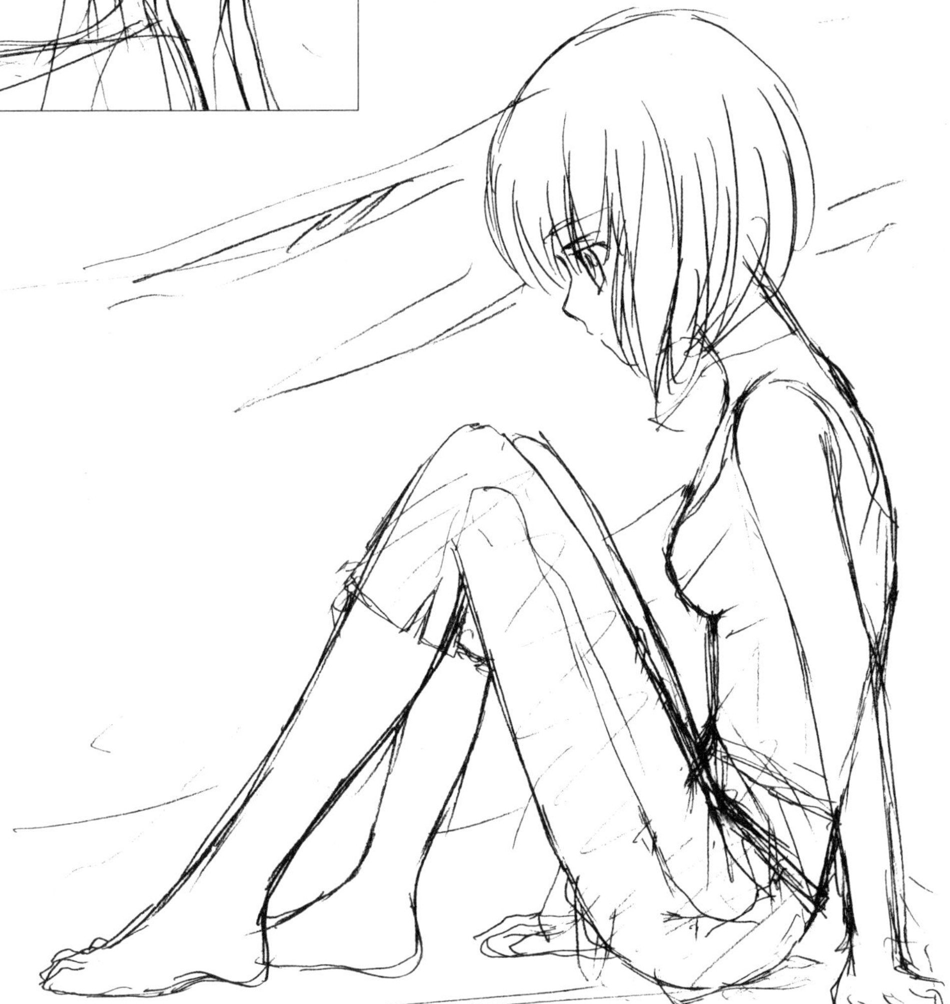

Meet a Real Kazuko Tadano Character

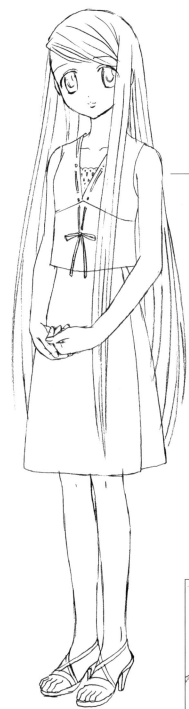

Alisa Nojima (age 22)

Alisa's parents raised her as they saw fit. Perhaps this is the reason she is a pliant, obedient girl, who has difficulty expressing herself. Alisa discovers that her parents have been discussing an arranged marriage for her without consulting Alisa on her intentions, causing her to have doubts about her situation. Alisa's true nature that she tucked away in a tiny corner inside herself begins to emerge bit by bit through the aid of Ellémeme. But, does the future hold happiness for Alisa?

—I had intended to show with this character that it is difficult to live through your own willpower. It seems like a simple task, and yet it is actually quite tricky. If someone is there, living seems easier, often taking away the need for worry. This is a character I conceived while doing some serious self-introspection.

Natsuki Kubo (age 27)

Natsuki is a certified financial planner with a managerial position. She wants to get married as much as anyone, but her stern personality and tendency to rush around seem to be getting in the way. She resorts to harsh language to hide her sensitivity, but no one seems to notice. Today yet again, we see Natsuki return home to her apartment and sadly begin to prepare dinner all alone.

—Superficially, Natsuki projects the image of a career woman skillfully performing a difficult job. However, Natsuki is actually quite home-oriented but refuses to accept this aspect of herself, she finds herself holding the short end of the stick. Natsuki tends to remind us of someone we perhaps know. It was this type of career-oriented woman that I designed her to resemble.

Ryo Hayama (age 15)

Ryo's parents divorced, so Ryo became recorded under his mother's family's official register. His mother then remarried, but Ryo had difficulty getting along with his stepfather, and ultimately ran away from home.

—One day to kill time, Ryo enters a store. Whilst there, he becomes suspected of theft. He flees the scene, hiding in the storeroom of the bakery where Karen works. I came to the realization that female characters occupied all of the supporting roles, so I added a guy (grin), opting for a boy with a background similar to Karen.

Here, I tried to portray an image I had visualized in colors with a "Japanese" feel. White represents the sublime, and yellow, light. Red represents passion. Green represents the unchanging. Blue is truth. And finally, black represents the darkness of being totally enshrouded. Japan's ancient language of color is exceedingly unique, seemingly rich in diversity, enabling us to describe the seasons or our emotions. Here, I selected six colors for the base and used them according to my own personal interpretation.

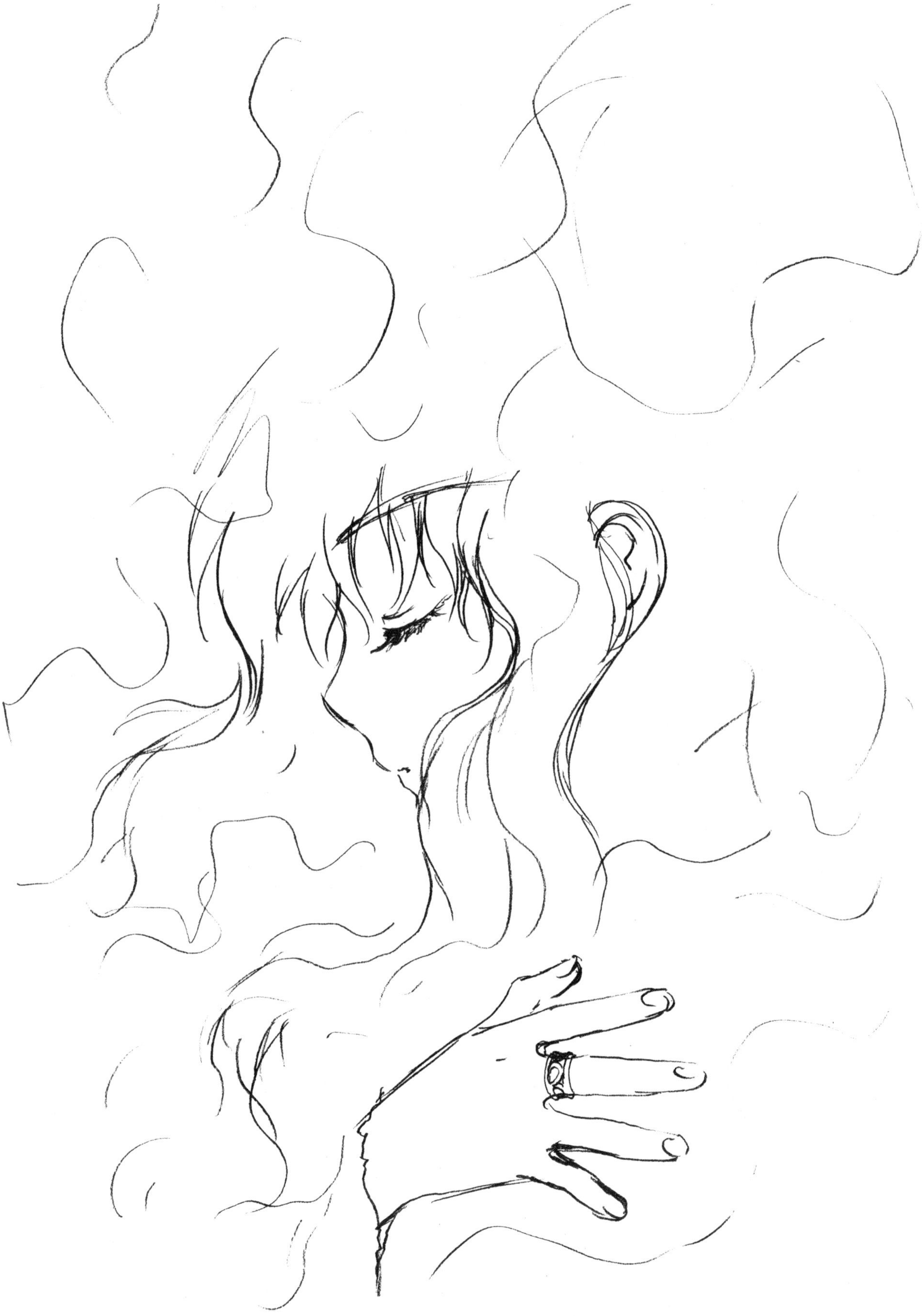

Black is a color that envelops all others, generating a sense of stillness and chaos. What does the Ellémeme dwelling in the niche of our darker selves think? What does she feel?

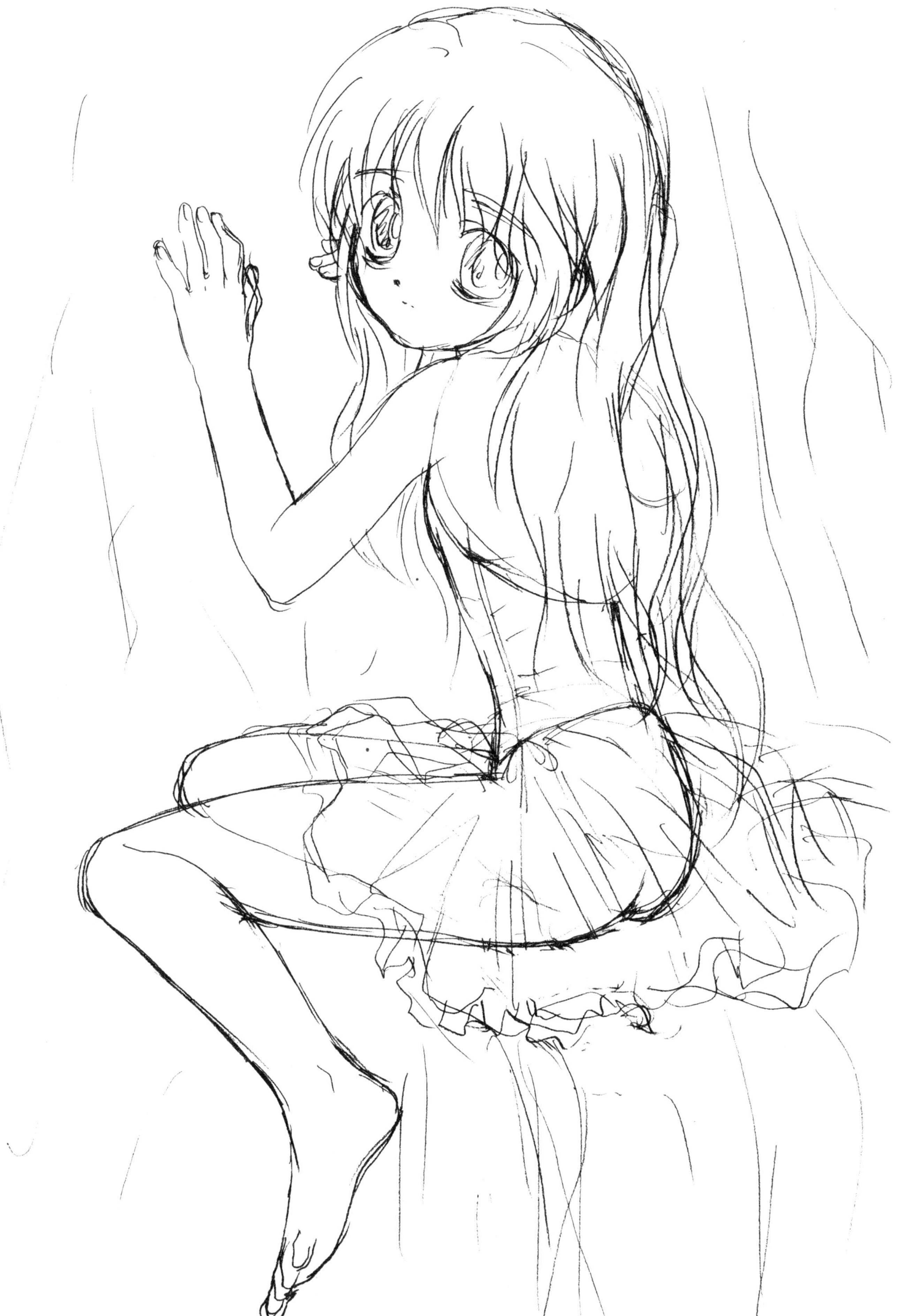

The figure seen on this page represents "blue." I used a pure "azure" to represent the truth. Cool, refreshing azure—the Ellémeme residing within this blue seeks a moment of truth.

Key Points in Producing Illustrations the Kazuko Tadano Way

Poses

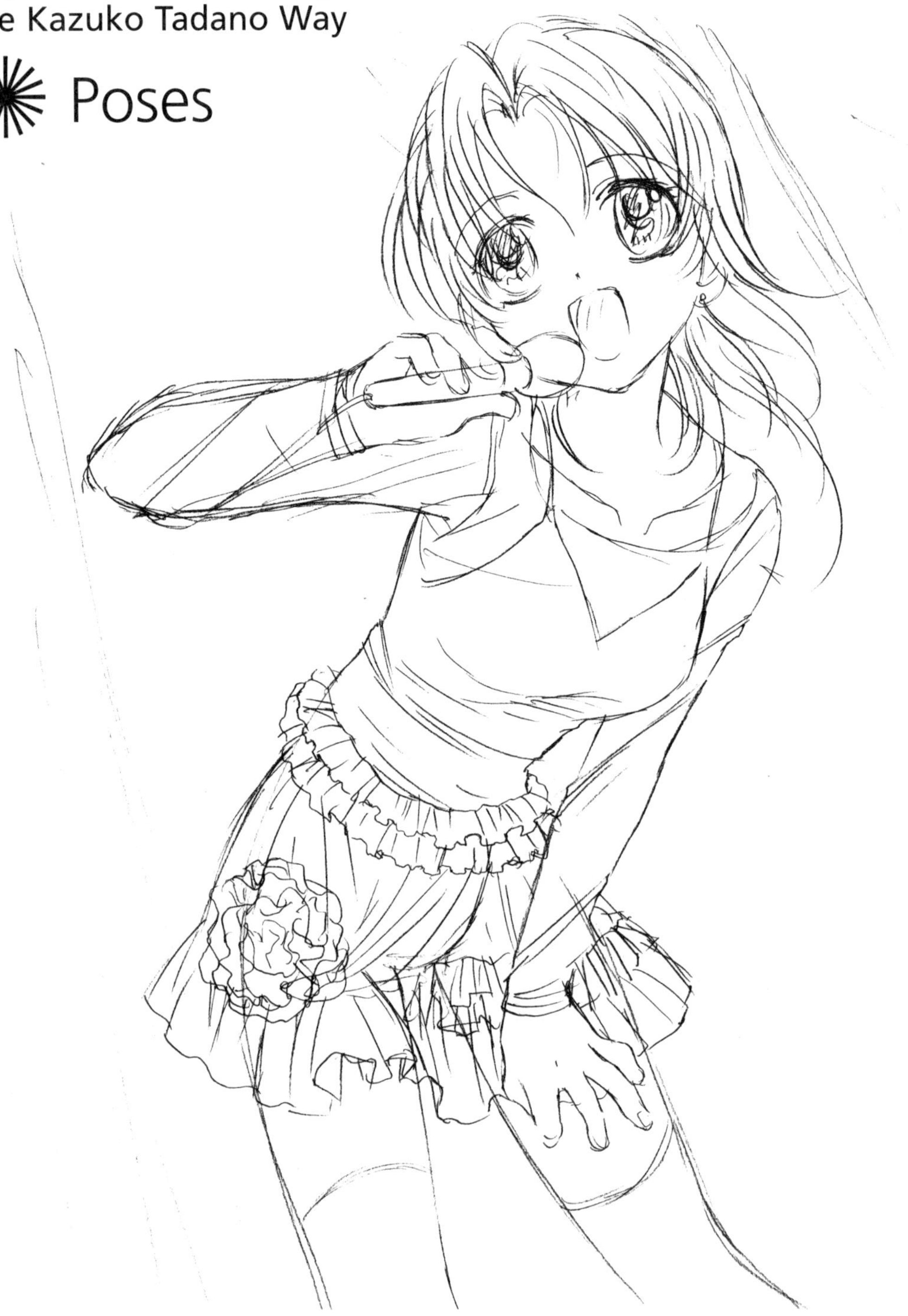

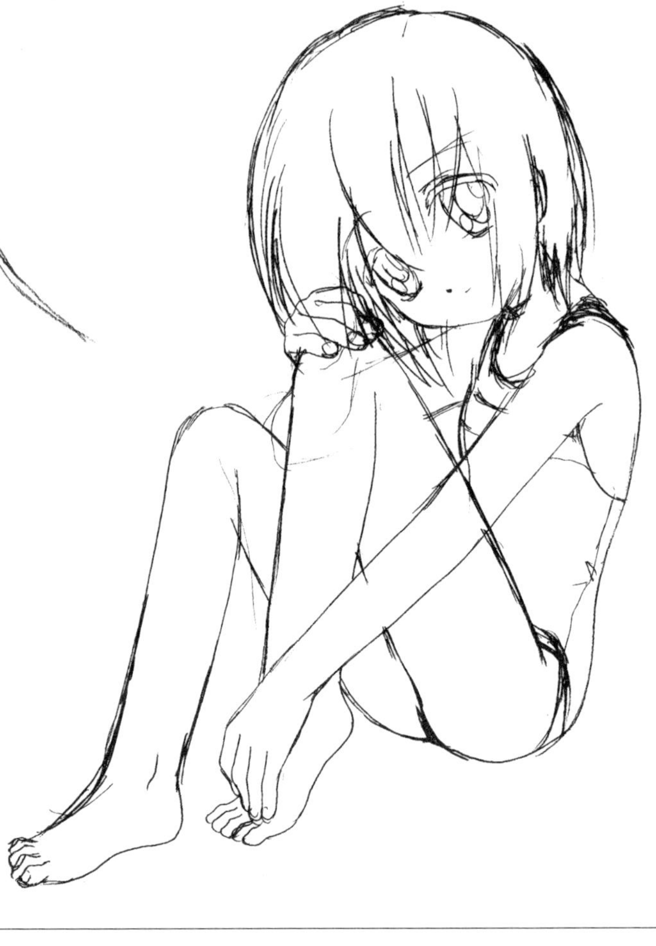

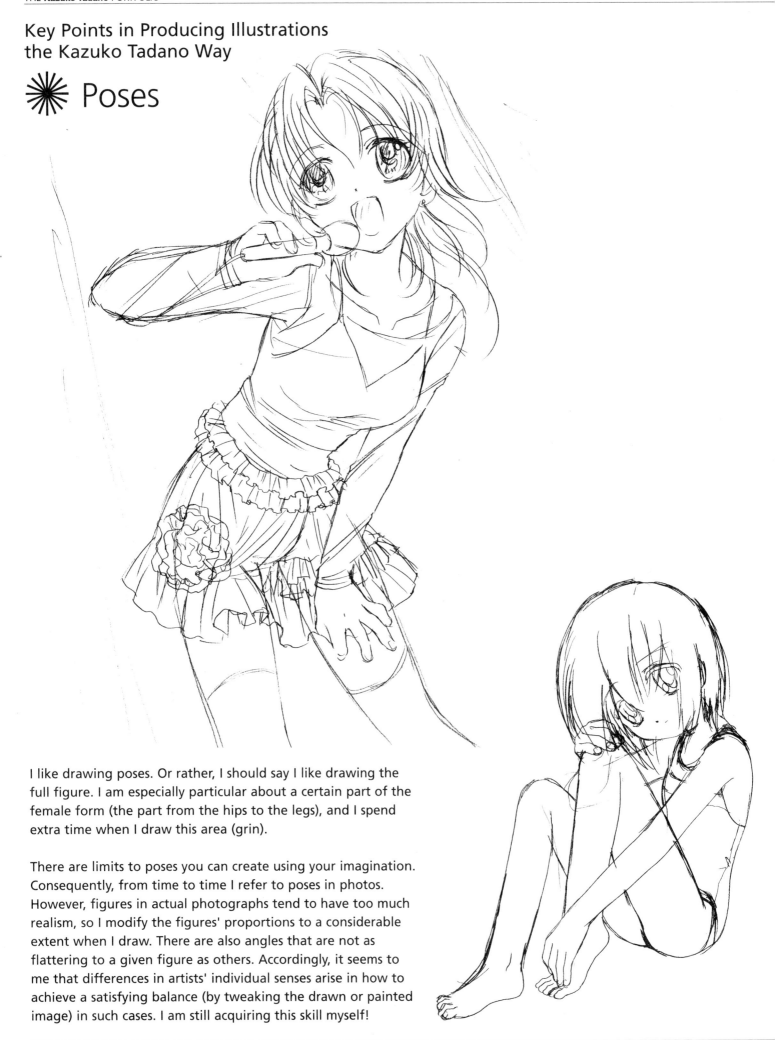

I like drawing poses. Or rather, I should say I like drawing the full figure. I am especially particular about a certain part of the female form (the part from the hips to the legs), and I spend extra time when I draw this area (grin).

There are limits to poses you can create using your imagination. Consequently, from time to time I refer to poses in photos. However, figures in actual photographs tend to have too much realism, so I modify the figures' proportions to a considerable extent when I draw. There are also angles that are not as flattering to a given figure as others. Accordingly, it seems to me that differences in artists' individual senses arise in how to achieve a satisfying balance (by tweaking the drawn or painted image) in such cases. I am still acquiring this skill myself!

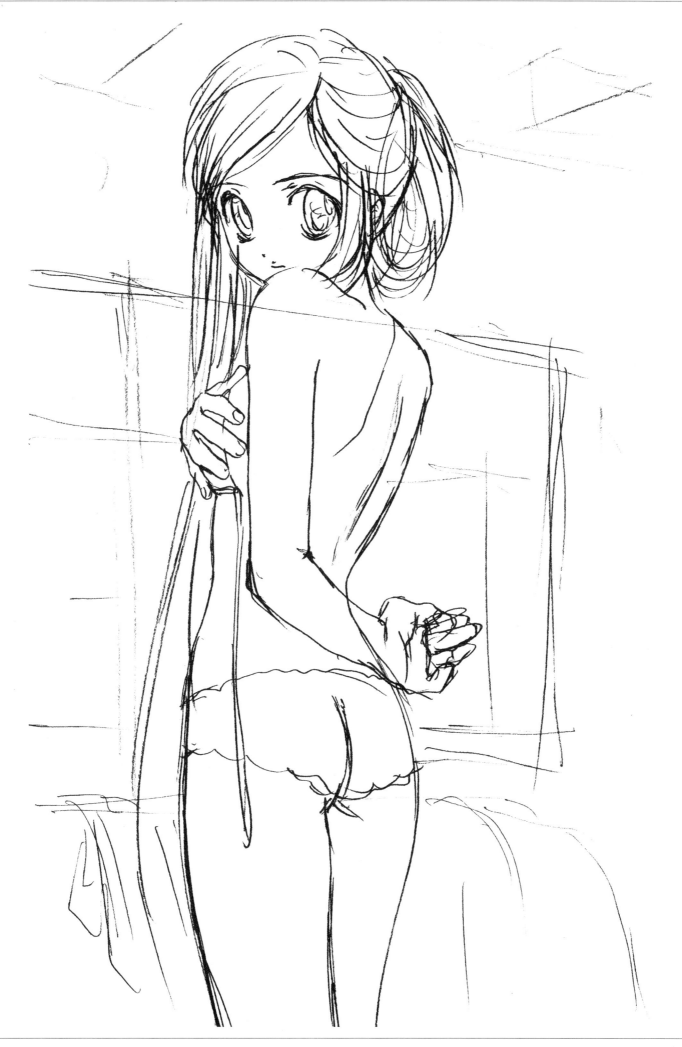

Key Points in Producing Illustrations the Kazuko Tadano Way

 The Composition

Layouts are incredibly difficult. In fact, I admit I'm still a bit uncomfortable with layouts (wry laugh). I tend to get caught up in debating whether I should have the character as the subject matter, since I'm going to the trouble of drawing the figure anyway, or I should have the background be the focus, placing the character within, but on a small scale.

In the figure to the right, the sky expands underneath Ellémeme's feet. The fluffy clouds look positively edible, but no matter how much you eat, you will never feel satisfied. Desire spreads without limit much like those clouds. It never runs out.

In the drawing of Alisa to the left, I transformed her innermost feelings into the backdrop. The countless flower petals float along the river. The petals never run against the current, but rather flow with it, thus portraying the heroine's personality in pictorial form.

The illustration on the next page depicts Miyu showing fear of her rivals. Although Miyu is not the lead character, I drew the rivals in the foreground larger, and positioned the trepid Miyu in the far ground. Switching around the positioning of a conventional composition conversely has the effect of drawing focus to the main character.

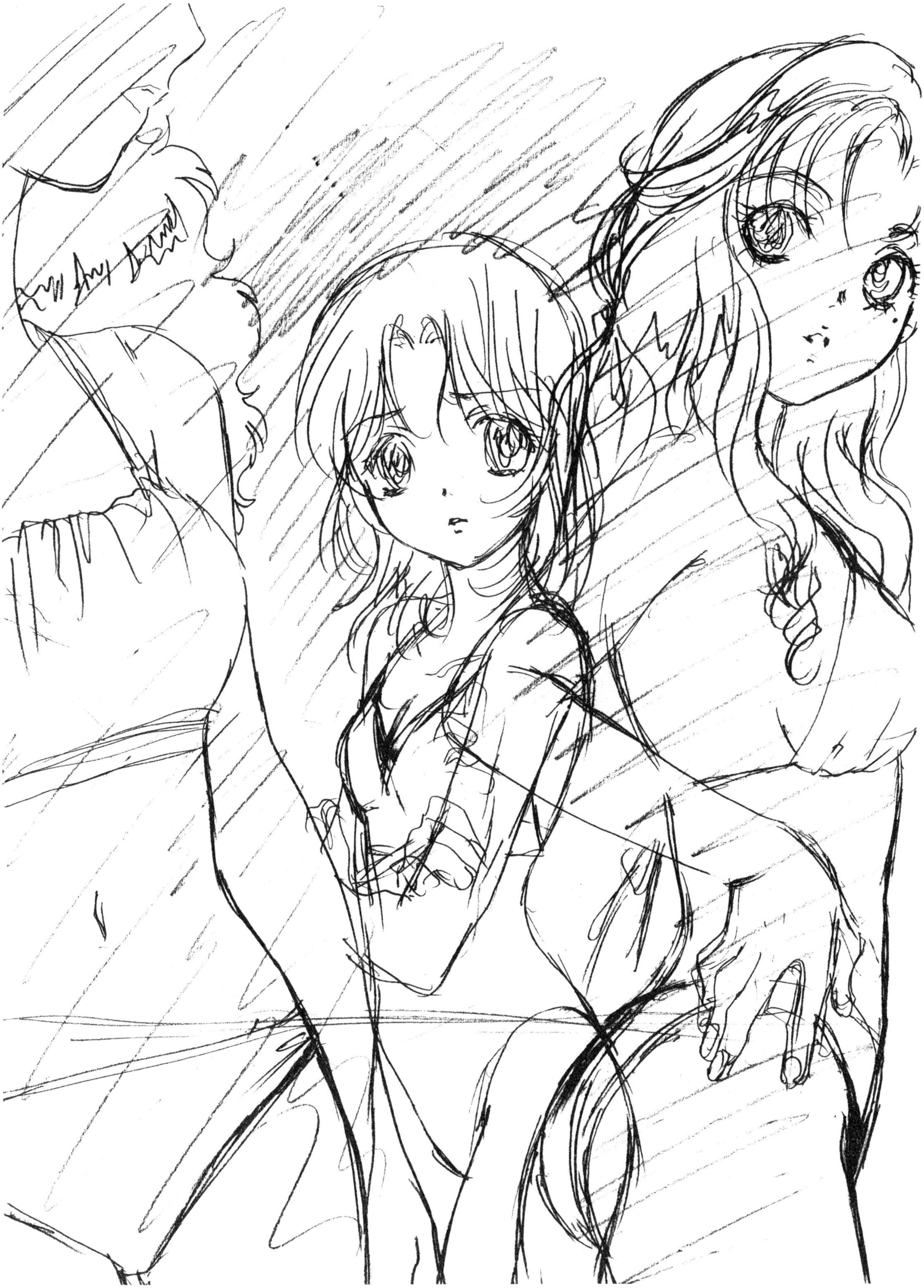

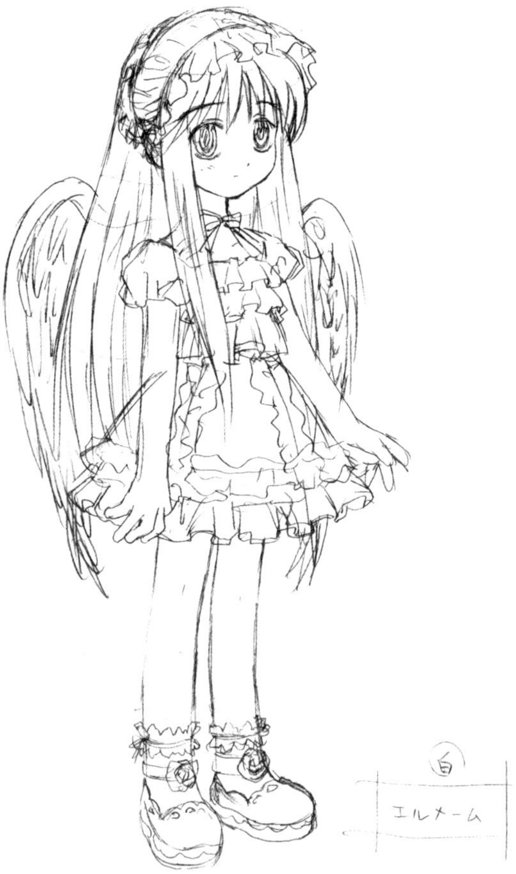
白
エルメーム

This rough sketch I drew for an *anime* project. While this character is not supposed to be an angel, I gave her wings to symbolize goodness and purity.

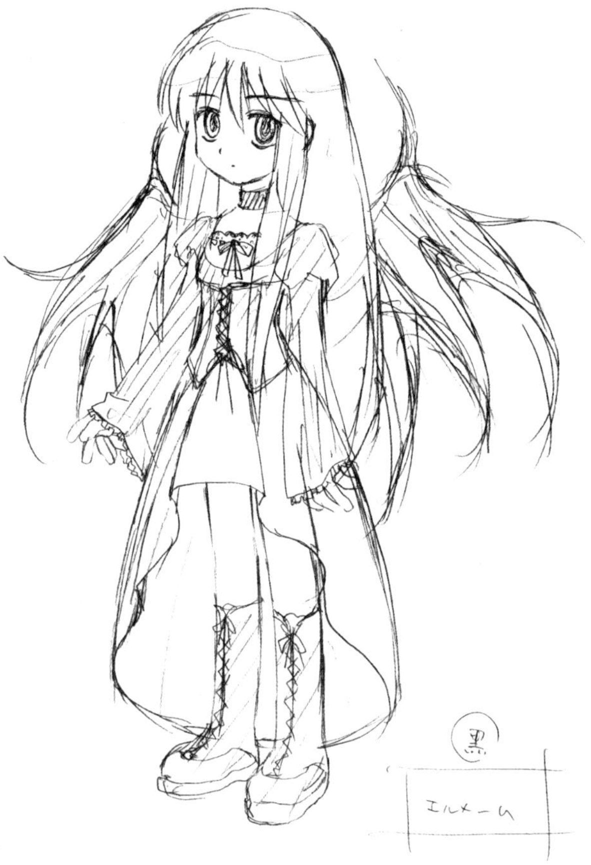
黒
エルメーム

This sketch is also for an *anime* project. Again, I gave this girl the type of wings shown to symbolize darkness.

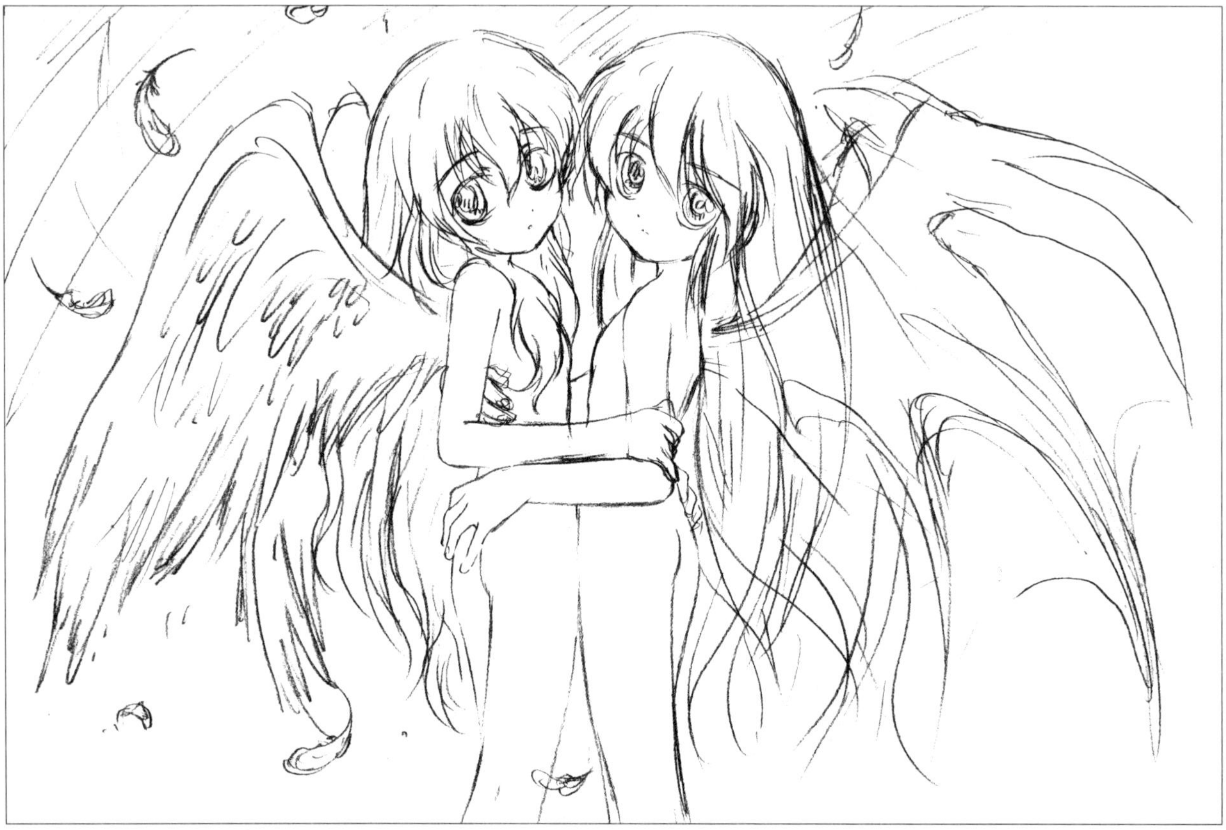

My theme for this drawing is 'Who will be chosen?" The two girls symbolize yin and yang. While they are nude, I tried to eliminate any suggestion of sexuality (chuckle). I paid careful attention to the wings' size and balance.

My theme for this drawing is "A Moment in Time." She is nude, because what you see is just the preliminary sketch. I do plan on dressing her. While I am a woman, I have great fun drawing girls' fannies (grin). I drew this composition from an overhead perspective, but I suspect I gave her body too much torsion. I doubt I could wrench myself into this pose.

My theme for this piece was "A Moment of Repose." In one sense, this common bed scene is almost an obligatory composition (smirk). I have not yet decided how to color the clothing (lingerie?). The balance of the overall layout did not work well vertically, so I composed it at an angle.

My theme for this drawing is "The Other Side of the Truth." I used an ancient-looking setting to pull this composition together. The girl, who stands on the boundary between the two worlds, displays elements of each. The walls are obscuring her wings, but I gave them a translucent feel.

This was intended to be a cover illustration. I wanted to show the character's full figure, so to prevent her from appearing overly tiny, I drew her seated. Girls around 10 years old have subtly rounded curves, which make them very difficult to draw.

Profile of Kazuko Tadano

■ Place of Birth: Hiroshima
 Zodiac Sign: Pisces
 Blood Type: B

Kazuko Tadano engaged in various activities (*anime*, magazine and book illustration, video games, *manga*, and assorted other genres) at her own studio, STUDIO VIEWN! Today, Kazuko Tadano continues to be active in a host of many projects.

■ **Filmography**

TV Series

Bishoujo Senshi Sailor Moon
(1992-1993; episodes 6, 12, 17, 21, 28, 34, 39, and 46)
—Character Design and Animation Director
 Be sure to catch episode 21! (Grin)

Bishoujo Senshi Sailor Moon R The Movie
(1993-1994; episodes 53, 58, 64, 69, and 88)
—Character Design and Animation Director

Choju Kishin Dankuga [*Super Bestial Machine God Dancougar*]
(1985-1986; episodes 4, 19, and 24):
—Character Design and Animation Director
 This is the first mechanical object artwork I have done!

Tongari Boshi no Memoru [*Pointy cap Memole*]
(1984-1985; episodes 5, 11, 17, 23, 29, 35, 40, 46)
—Animation Director

Mister Ajikko (episodes 19 and 25)
—Animation Director

Kingyo Chuiho [*Goldfish Warning*]
(episodes 14, 19, 25, 30, 35, 43, and 50)
—Animation Director

Majin Eiyuden Wataru [*Wataru Demon Sagas*] (episode 40)
—Animation Director

Saint Seiya (Episode 65)
—Animation Director

Cho'on Senshi Boguman [*Sonic Warrior Borgman*]
—Animation Director

I only worked on *Seiya* and *Borgman* on a single occasion in conjunction with one another—sort of unusual, given my past track record, wouldn't you say?

High School Kimengumi (episode 45)
—Animation Director

Step Jun (episodes 29 and 34)
—Animation Director

Aitenshi Densentsu Wedding Peach
[*Legend of the Angel of Love, Wedding Peach*] (1995)
—Character Design

Puchi Puri Yucie (2002)
—Character Design and Animation Director for intro(OP)

Videos

Crystal Triangle
—Character Design and Animation Director

Choju Kishin Dankuga: Ushinawareta monotachi e no chinkonka
[*Super Bestial Machine God Dancougar: Requiem to Victims*]
—Character Design and Animation Director

Sotsugyo [*Graduation*]
—Character Design and Animation Director

Cinematic Features

Bishoujo Senshi Sailor Moon R The Movie (1993)
—Character Design and Animation Director

Choro Q Dougram (1983)
—Character Design and Animation Director

Publications

Kazuko Tadano Illustrations Favorite!!
MOVIC
—First illustration collection!

Star Pinky Q (vol. 1)
Media Works Inc.
Star Pinky Q (vol. 2)
Media Works Inc.

Produced the artwork for a series published in the monthly periodical *Gao* with Minda Nao (story)

AYUS The Second Seimeitai [*Secondary Life form AYUS*] (vol. 1)
Kadokawa Shoten Publishing Co., Ltd.

AYUS The Second Seimeitai [*Secondary Life form AYUS*] (vol. 2)
Kadokawa Shoten Publishing Co., Ltd.
—First original *manga*, published as a series in *Shonen Ace*

HOW TO DRAW MANGA: Girls' Life Illustration File
Graphic-sha Publishing Co., Ltd.
—Original character illustration guide

Games and Software

Shin Seikoku La Wars (1995)
Shindosha
—Character Design

NEC PC-FX Software (1995)
—Designed the flagship character Rolfee

NEC PC-FX Software (1997): *Tonari no Princess Rolfee* [*Rolfee, the Princess Next Door*]
NEC Home Electronics Ltd.
—First game produced

Rolfee Screensaver for Windows 95 (1997)
NEC Home Electronics Ltd.

The Love Adventure *Okaeri*! An Evening Calm-flavored Love Story Game for Windows (released Feb. 21, 2001)
—Original drawing
Arco Entertainment

The Love Adventure *Okaeri*! An Evening Calm-flavored Love Story Game for Sony PlayStation (released Dec. 20, 2001)
D3 Publisher Inc.

The Love Adventure *Okaeri*! An Evening Calm-flavored Love Story Game for Sega Dreamcast (released Sept. 26, 2002)
D3 Publisher Inc.
Both ported from the PC version

CDs

CD Drama Series *Star Pinky Q* (CONTACT 1): *Uchu Shojo Tokyo ni Arawaru* [*Space Girls Appear in Tokyo*]
MediaRing Ltd. and Polygram
—Illustration for use in packaging

CD Drama Series *Star Pinky Q* (CONTACT 2): *Yusei Majin Getsumen no Akumu* [*Planetary Demons: Nightmare on the Moon's Surface*]
MediaRing Ltd. and Polygram
—Illustration for use in packaging

CD Drama Series *Star Pinky Q* Soundtrack
MediaRing Ltd. and Polygram
—Illustration for use in packaging

NEC PC-FX *Tonari no Princess* [*The Princess Next Door*]
Ayers and Bandai Music Entertainment Inc.
—Opening and ending music lyric writer